BOOK OF ROSES

Frontispiece Floribunda, Glacier.

HOME GARDEN BOOK OF
Roses

BY THE STAFF OF **HOME GARDEN'S** NATURAL GARDENING MAGAZINE

CHARLES SCRIBNER'S SONS   NEW YORK

PHOTOGRAPHIC CREDITS

Molly Adams, p. 129; *A. Devaney, Inc.*, p. 78 (C); *Paul E. Genereux*, p. 19 (top left), 56, 63; *Gottscho-Schleisner*, p. 7 (right), 22 (both), 54, 59, 61, 64, 65, 72, 163 (top left); *Jeannette Grossman*, p. 50; *Hampfler*, p. 139 (bottom); *Arthur Heitzman*, p. 163 (bottom left and right); *M. C. Ohlander*, p. 93; *Roche*, p. 3, 14 (both), 19 (top right, bottom left and right), 24, 86, 154, 163 (top right); *John J. Simpkins*, p. 78 (A, E), 79, 107 (right).

Armstrong Nurseries, p. viii; *The Conard-Pyle Company*, p. 30, 32, 42 (right), 76 (left), 139 (top); *Germain's*, p. 10; *Howards of Hemet, California*, p. 82; *Jackson & Perkins Company*, p. ii, 7 (left), 28, 33 (right), 38, 69, 76 (right), 78 (B, D), 80 (right), 123 (both), 161, 167, 171.

COLOR PLATES

Plate 1 Command Performance, *All America Rose Selections*
Plate 2 White Knight, Golden Prince, *The Conard-Pyle Company*
Plate 3 Camelot, Mister Lincoln, *The Conard-Pyle Company*
Plate 4 Chrysler Imperial, Lady Elgin, *The Conard-Pyle Company*
Plate 5 Peace, *Natural Gardening Magazine (Mrs. Virginia Rafool)*
Plate 6 Queen Elizabeth, *The Conard-Pyle Company*
Aquarius, *All America Rose Selections*
Taj Mahal, *Armstrong Nurseries, Inc.*
Plate 7 Scarlet Knight, Fashion, *The Conard-Pyle Company*
Red Gold, *All America Rose Selections*
Plate 8 Fire King, Rhonda, *The Conard-Pyle Company*
Sonoma, *Armstrong Nurseries, Inc.*

A–10.72(Q)

Published in the United States of America
Library of Congress Catalog Card Number 73–39334
SBN 684–12908–6 (trade cloth)

CONTENTS

LIST OF COLOR PLATES

Circus.

1

WHAT KIND OF ROSE FOR YOU?

Of course you *love* roses; who does not? In America as in most of the world, it is the genus *Rosa* that is favored above all others. Actually, no other plant has been so celebrated in song and story, art and literature, and, more to the point, in the gardens of flower lovers all over the world.

The first record of the wild rose was found on fragments of a Bronze Age fresco on the island of Crete. Roses were grown in Egypt for the Mediterranean trade in attar and flowers for garlands, chaplets, and deep piles of rose petals that made Roman orgies worthy of the name. *Rosa rugosa* was treasured a thousand years ago by the emperors of China and Japan, and the Provins rose, among others, was tended in medieval cloisters.

A regal patron of the rose was Empress Josephine. With her knowledge and enthusiasm, and Napoleon's income, the Empress directed the planting of an incomparable garden at Malmaison on the outskirts of Paris. Every rose known to man was planted there; then André Dupont was commanded to create others. He had been cross-pollinating carnations with considerable success and soon developed techniques for hybridizing roses that are used today.

Another important contribution to interest in the flower was the commissioning of the artist Pierre Joseph Redoute to depict the roses of Malmaison. In stipple engraving and color he produced *Les Roses*, a book of some seven hundred exquisite portraits that are yet unsurpassed.

The rose through the ages has been used as a synonym for truth, honor,

1

the blushing cheek, and lips of red. But it was Gertrude Stein who put it in perspective. "A rose," she said, "is a rose is a rose." To know what it is and to understand why it is so revered, one need only look at the flower. Some of the species have the guileless appeal of the daisy. Bright face to the world, form crisp, color clear. Tea roses, *centifolias*, and the others of full form are more evocative. Color varies from the light-touched edges to deepest shadow, always suffused with the hue of the petals.

There is in the unfolding of a rose the intriguing mystery of what lies within, and the subtle promise of beauty yet to come. On the pages that follow is all you need to know to enjoy these beguiling plants in your own garden.

CLASSIFICATION OF ROSES

Roses are generally classified into groups according to similarity in habit of growth, form of flower, hardiness, and other characteristics. Actually, however, there is no sharp line of difference among all of the various types, because plant breeders have crossed and recrossed varieties from different sections until many modern roses now possess characteristics from two or more groups. Nevertheless, the roses now generally recognized as belonging to one group have many characteristics in common and also respond to the same general cultural practices. Practically all rose catalogs now list rose varieties under these recognized groups. The beginning rose fancier needs an understanding of the differences among groups so he can select precisely the varieties he wishes to grow.

There are two main classes of roses—bush roses and climbing roses. These two classes are based entirely on habit of growth. Bush roses grow from 1 to 6 feet in height and require no support. Climbing roses produce long canes each year and must be provided with some type of support.

Figure 1 (*right*) The hybrid tea, Peace—one of the most famous roses of all times—in a garden setting.

BUSH ROSES

Bush roses include many types grouped according to flowering habit, winter hardiness, and other traits. These types are hybrid teas, floribundas, polyanthas, grandifloras, hybrid perpetuals, old-fashioned roses, shrub roses, and tree or standard roses.

Hybrid Teas

Hybrid teas are more widely grown and more popular than all other types of roses combined. They are the so-called monthly or everblooming roses, and are the ones grown in beds in rose gardens and by florists under glass. In fact, when the word "rose" is used, it generally suggests a hybrid tea variety.

The first hybrid tea was introduced in France in 1867. It was a cross between two older roses—the hybrid perpetual, which dominated the rose world from 1840 to 1890, and the tea rose, a vigorous, everblooming hybrid that was imported from China in the eighteenth century—and the product was called *La France*. It was the beginning of a great era in the history of the rose.

That era loomed even bigger when the plant patent act in the United States gave impetus to plant breeding. This was in 1932. Hybridizers and nurserymen have been producing new roses ever since. Each year sees dozens of new good hybrid teas. The range of colors is constantly expanding. The other qualities of a good rose are being added—lovelier foliage, for example, or disease resistance. In fact, in recent years the story of the rose is the story of the hybridists and commercial growers who, with infinite patience and insight, have created, grown, and marketed today's magnificent array of roses. The hybridizer chooses two plants for particular characteristics he wants to combine and adds the pollen from one to the stigmas of the other; he harvests the resulting seed and plants it with great expectations. Each of the thousands of seedlings produced by a cross is carefully studied, and the few with promise are further tested.

In Germany, the houses of Kordes and Tantau have developed some famous varieties. At Lyon, France, Francis Meilland of the rose-growing family has created many great ones including Peace, the most popular rose of all time. In this country, the famous names are Walter Lammerts, Herbert C. Swim, and

4

the late Eugene Boerner. When the promising seedlings of new crosses have been grown under varied conditions in test gardens all across the country and have passed the critical standards established by the growers, they are ready to produce commercially. New hybrids are grafted (budded) on to the sturdy vigorous rootstock of *Rosa multiflora.* A bud and sliver of bark are carefully cut from the new variety, slipped into the rootstock, and bound to seal the union.

Most hybrid teas are winter-hardy in the milder sections of the country, but varieties differ in cold resistance. In sections where winters are severe, practically all varieties need some protection. The plants grow from about 18 to 20 inches or more, depending on the culture, type of pruning, and climatic conditions. The flowers vary from singles that have but one row of petals to doubles with many rows. In general, the buds are pointed and long, and the flowers are borne one to a stem or in clusters of three to five.

Hybrid tea varieties exist in a wide range of colors, including pure white and many shades of red, yellow, pink, and orange. Imagine, if you will, a tremendous color board, with many shades of each of these colors on it. In fact, there would be many more colors: deep midnight reds, lavenders, tans, coffees, even chartreuse. Never quite a blue—but everything else. Imagine any beautiful fabric you have ever seen, a sunset, or any subtle shading of several tones —a coral peach, a gray and lavender. No matter what you imagine, or what you look at on your color board, hybrid teas exist that are just as wonderful, just as subtle, just as unusual. An iridescent red, for example, with golden stamens can be found in some of the new ones.

The first use for hybrid teas that comes to mind is cutting—for loose display in informal vases or for more carefully staged arrangements. The many modern colors in today's homes need new colors in roses to set them off, to complement their boldness. But the hybrid tea makes an impressive display when growing; it is a conversation piece, blooms from June until late fall, and has many flower forms and many new qualities.

Most hybrid teas have some fragrance. This characteristic, however, is variable; some varieties are very fragrant and others only slightly fragrant. When fragrance is present, it is usually more intense in the early morning before the fragrant oil has evaporated from the base of the petals.

Here are some of tried and true hybrid tea favorites—starting with reds: Crimson Glory, Charlotte Armstrong, Chrysler Imperial, Tallyho, Rubaiyat, Christopher Stone, Etoile de Hollande, Grande Duchesse Charlotte, Nocturne, New Yorker, Mirandy, Texas Centennial, Mister Lincoln, Oklahoma, Christian

Dior, Lotte Gunthart, Tropicana, Otto Miller, Fragrant Cloud, Pharaoh, Big Red, and Indiana.

Among the pinks are Dainty Bess, First Love, The Doctor, Picture, Radiance, Rubaiyat, Capistrano, Bewitched, Royal Highness, South Sea, Courtship, Pink Favorite, Elsa Knoll, Show Girl, Duet, Pink Peace, Confidence, Laura, and Candy Stripe.

The whites include White Wings, Pedralbes, McGredy's Ivory, Pascali, Matterhorn, White Knight, Snowbird, Blanche Mallerin, Garden Party, Dresden, Happy Wedding Bells, Sweet Afton, and John F. Kennedy.

The yellows include Golden Wings, Eclipse, Lowell Thomas, King's Ransom, Lemon Elegance, Summer Sunshine, Golden Gate, Soeur Therese, Golden Prince, and Apollo.

The blends—some subtle, some the striking bicolors—include Peace, Tiffany, Helen Traubel, Good News, President Herbert Hoover, Sutter's Gold, American Heritage, Garden Party, Mme Henri Guillot, Confidence, Lafter Saturnia, Tip Toes, Mission Bells, Summer Rainbow, American Heritage, Chicago Peace, Swarthmore, Colorama, Condesa de Sastago, Fragrant Cloud, Granada, Lady X, and Polynesian Sunset.

There are thousands of other hybrid teas on the market, and new ones are introduced each year. Any one of them could be *your* favorite. More on the selection of hybrid teas will be found in the next chapter.

Floribundas

Floribunda roses—introduced in 1924—are a modern horticultural development produced from crossing hybrid teas with polyantha roses. The everblooming habit and wide color range of the hybrid teas and the hardiness and disease resistance of the polyanthas are apparent in their make-up. In recent years, rose hybridizers have developed much larger and fuller flowers as well.

The range of flower forms is wide. There are perfect singles, such as Fairy Cluster, and doubles, such as Red Pinocchio. In addition, a few of the taller types, notably Geranium Red, produce single flowers to a stem as well as flowers in clusters. Aside from their vitality, the floribundas thrive under a wider range of temperatures and soil types than any other roses. Originally produced in Denmark and Holstein in answer to the need for roses for cold areas, they grow equally well, perhaps even better, in temperate and often very hot areas.

6

Floribundas are of upright form, growing from 2 to 4 feet tall, or more, making them suitable for many decorative purposes. Generally the bushes are compact, with the abundant foliage making a splendid setting for the flowers. The blossoms are produced in clusters on strong, stiff stems, which makes them ideal for garden display or indoor decoration. Another pleasing feature of this type of rose is the way the flowers develop—they do not all open at the same time, thus prolonging the period of bloom. Floribunda blossoms are among the longest lasting flowers, both on the bush or when cut. They definitely belong to the group known as "good keepers."

Figure 2 Two all-time popular floribundas: Red Pinocchio *(left)*, and Pink Chiffon.

The perfectly shaped buds, gems for corsages and arrangements, are a bonus feature of the floribundas. It is possible to cut blooms from such varieties as Pink Rosette and Crimson Rosette with stems 24 to 30 inches long. Frequently one cluster of a half-dozen or more perfectly shaped buds makes an entire bouquet. The flowers are just as beautiful when fully open as in buds, and some, such as Fashion, are even more attractive in the advanced stages of flower development.

Following are lists of some of the all-time favorites among floribundas:

RED	PINK	WHITE
Red Pinocchio	Betty Prior	Dagmar Spath
Eutin	Pink Bountiful	Summer Snow
Frensham	Rosenolfe	Iceberg
Pied Piper	Tom Tom	Ivory Fashion
Spartan	Else Poulsen	Ice White
Cocorico	Betsy McCall	Saratoga
Donald Prior	Pinocchio	
Floradora	Lilibet	BLENDS
Ginger	Pink Chiffon	Fashion
Wildfire	Frolic	Little Darling
Permanent Wave	Gene Boerner	Vogue
World's Fair		Circus
Fire King		Ma Perkins
Europeana	YELLOW	Circus Parade
Sarabande	Yellow Cushion	Masquerade
Geranium Red	Gold Cup	Jiminy Cricket
Garnette	Goldilocks	Roman Holiday
Tamango	Allgold	Apricot Nectar
	Starlet	Ginger
	Sunpat	Angel Face
		Redgold Rumba

More on the selection of floribundas will be found in Chapter 2.

Polyanthas

Polyantha roses are distinguished from the floribundas by their smaller flowers, which are borne in large clusters. They are closely related to many of the climbing roses, having flower clusters very similar to them in form and size of individual florets. The polyanthas are hardy and may be grown in many sections where hybrid teas are difficult to grow. Their chief use is in bed plantings or in borders with other perennials. They are excellent for mass plantings. However, the best mass color effects are obtained if the bushes are planted from 15 to 18 inches apart in beds with several plants of the same variety grouped together. Care should be taken, however, that the colors of adjacent groups form a pleasing harmony or contrast and that plants of similar growth are grouped together. The dwarf forms are useful for borders and for the edging of beds, while the taller varieties are essentially bedders.

With but very few exceptions, both the small- and the large-flowered types are vigorous and robust. Basal shoots are freely produced on both, though less so on the large-flowered than on the small-flowered. Both are exceedingly free-flowering and, as the individual flowers in each cluster open in succession, the display of color is prolonged.

The color range is quite comprehensive, ranging from white through all gradations of flesh, rose, cerise, and carmine to orange-scarlet and crimson. Fragrance, unfortunately, is sadly lacking in most of the polyanthas, although this deficiency is not a serious fault in a bedding rose. Nevertheless, the rose has a reputation to uphold in this respect, and eventually we may expect more fragrant polyanthas.

As the primary purpose of these roses is to provide masses of color and the size of the individual blossoms is of secondary importance, pruning should be held to a minimum. It should consist only of the removal of dead or weak wood and the shortening of too robust growth. An occasional thinning out is advisable, however, if the growth becomes too dense. Greater flower production may be induced by the removal of faded flowers, but they will bloom generously enough without such treatment. They will thrive on neglect, but they will also well repay any special attention given them in the way of cultivation and feeding.

Some of the better varieties of polyanthas still available are:

Cameo	Light salmon
Chatillion	Light pink
Cecile Brunner	Light pink
China Doll	Pink
Eglantine	Pink
Gloria Mundi	Orange-scarlet
Mrs. R. M. Finch	Pink
The Fairy	Pink

9

Grandifloras

A comparatively new class of roses, grandifloras are produced from crosses between the hybrid teas and floribundas. In most instances, they combine the best features of both parents. Flowers, which are borne both in clusters and singly on long stems, are slightly smaller than hybrid tea blossoms, but they share the same perfection of bud and flower form. Normally, grandifloras are big plants and need plenty of space in the garden. Some varieties are upright in habit and grow to well over 6 feet high, while others are hefty plants 3 feet or more in diameter. Most grandifloras have vigorous growth, hardiness, ever-blooming habits, and the disease resistance of their grandparents—the polyantha rose.

Since grandifloras were not introduced until the late 1940s, the number of truly *popular* varieties is still somewhat limited. The best known ones are:

Camelot	Coral-pink
John S. Armstrong	Dark red
Queen Elizabeth	Pink
Carrousel	Dark red
Comanche	Salmon-orange
Montezuma	Burnt orange
Golden Girl	Yellow
Pink Parfait	Pink blend
Roundelay	Red
Starfire	Red
Scarlet Knight	Red
Mount Shasta	White
Lucky Lady	Pink
Aquarius	Pink
Starburst	Red-yellow
Granada	Red blend
Olé	Red
Apricot Nectar	Apricot blend
El Capitan	Red

Hybrid Perpetuals

Hybrid perpetuals are the June roses of "great grandmother's" garden. Actually, this class of rose forms a link between the roses of the early part of the nineteenth century and those of today. The flowers are massive in comparison to the

Figure 3 The first grandiflora to receive the AARS award was the Queen Elizabeth.

hybrid tea roses and the plants are exceptionally vigorous and somewhat hardier. The June bloom is freely produced and a few varieties repeat sparingly later in the summer. In early spring all vigorous growth should be cut back to 1 or 2 feet from the ground and all weak, old, or dead canes should be removed entirely. These roses are gross feeders. They are very hardy and stand low winter temperatures without protection.

Some of the better varieties are:

General Jacqueminot	Red to crimson
Ulrich Brunner	Red to crimson
Henry Nevard	Red to crimson
Magna Charta	Red to crimson
American Beauty	Rose-red
Baroness Rothschild	Pink
Mrs. John Laing	Pink
Paul Neyron	Pink
Frau Karl Druschki	White
Roger Lambelin	Red to crimson
Prince Camille de Rohan	Red to crimson
Fisher Holmes	Red to crimson

Old-Fashioned Roses

During the centuries that the rose has reigned as queen of the flower world, several distinct types have attained popularity—each in its turn considered the acme of rose perfection. Yet many of the original species roses and old favorites possess desirable attributes that are not found in the modern varieties. If their assets were more widely known, old-fashioned or grandmother's roses would rival the new in popularity.

Even the most ardent admirer of old-fashioned roses realizes that they are not equipped to replace our present-day favorites, but they can be used advantageously with the hybrid teas, floribundas, and climbers. What is more, they take part with considerable poise in an overall landscape scheme where the finest hybrid tea would be at a loss. Collectors' items though the species roses may be— and a joy as such to the hobbyist—they have the true aristocrat's ability to mix companionably with more common garden inhabitants. Fortunately, garden designers and commercial rose growers are beginning to appreciate their qualities, and the better of the species of old roses are now more readily obtainable.

12

These more primitive roses should be classed as shrubs rather than bedding plants; when compared with other shrubs their worth becomes apparent. In addition to possessing certain sentimental and genealogical value, they are, as a whole, dependably hardy, disease resistant, and tolerant of soil and environment —and downright attractive, too.

Since they differ considerably in stature, habit, and blossom color, many have utilitarian as well as esthetic traits. Some are ideal subjects for accent points in the shrub border or foundation planting, as well as for individual specimens. Others may be used to conceal an unsightly view, to form an impregnable hedge, to prevent erosion, or for naturalizing. Against a picket fence, along a drive, grouped in the center of a turnabout, as a pair of slightly bristly sentinels at the entrance gate—wherever there is sun these roses will hold their own as stars or sturdy supporters in the garden scheme. Some of the taller kinds make an ideal background for a birdbath; smaller ones complement a sundial.

The majority bloom but once a year; still, the flowering period is long and profuse. In many instances the blossoms are followed by brightly colored fruits or hips that add greatly to the autumn beauty of the garden and contribute to indoor bouquets. A planting of these roses invariably increases the bird population in a garden; they find the thorny branches a safe and desirable nesting place, and they are fond of the fruits.

Old-fashioned roses require no more attention than other shrubs. An annual springtime removal of dead and exceedingly old wood and cutting back too rampant growth will suffice. More severe pruning may increase the size of individual blooms, but there will be fewer flowers, and in many instances an unpruned plant is far more attractive than a tailored one.

The following are the more popular and most readily available classes of old-fashioned roses:

CHINA ROSES

The two original members of the China rose group (*Rosa chinensis*) reached England in 1789 and were the first dependable everblooming roses known in Europe. Their introduction was the beginning of a new era in the rose world and to their influence must be credited all of the modern roses that bloom throughout the summer. They are somewhat more hardy than the hybrid teas, but require protection in the North. Pruning should consist of removing all dead and very old wood. Fertilize them heavily.

13

Figure 4 Two species of Grandmother's roses: *(left) Rosa spinosissima* (Scotch Brier), and *Rosa chinensis* (Old Blush).

China roses are difficult to obtain. In fact only about three variations—Old Blush (pink), Cramoise Superieur (red), and Ducher (white)—are available commercially.

TEA ROSES

Tea roses are truly the aristocrats of the rose world. Unfortunately they are gradually being supplanted by their progeny, the hybrid teas, which are somewhat hardier and available in a greater range of colors. The tea rose foliage is held more tenaciously than that of the hybrid teas, but the flower stem is often weak and the buds have a tendency to ball and rot during extremely wet weather.

14

Pruning should be moderate and should consist only of removing dead and weak growth. These roses do best in well drained fertile soil, and require adequate winter protection in the North.

A few of the better known varieties are:

Mme Lombard ....Rose-salmon
Safrano ....Yellow
Duchesse de Brabant ....Pink
Catherine Mermet ....Pink
Maman Cochet ....Pink
Sombreuil ....White

HYBRID MUSKS

The various members of the hybrid musk group range in height from 3 feet to 8 feet and bear their single to double flowers in clusters. (The true musk rose, *Rosa moschata*, is not available today.) They bloom throughout the summer but are at their best in late summer and autumn. Although hybrid musk roses are quite hardy where temperatures do not fall below zero, pruning should be rather severe as they bloom best on new wood. Early bloom is sacrificed by severe pruning, but the strong basal shoots encouraged by this are so loaded with buds that the late summer bloom production is tremendous.

Of the hybrid musks that are commercially available, the following are the favorites:

Clytemnestra ....Salmon
Belinda ....Pink
Kathleen ....Pink
Penelope ....Pink
Francis E. Lester ....Pink to white
White Prosperity ....White
R. Nastarana ....White
Rosaleen ....Red

SWEETBRIER

The Sweetbrier (*Rosa eglanteria*) has no rival in the garden for sweet scents. As its name implies, it is the foliage of this rose that is fragrant. From early spring, when the young curling leaves first appear on the sprouting branches,

15

until Jack Frost withers the leaves in the fall, this fragrance fills the garden. It is especially delightful following a spring or summer shower or in the early morning when the foliage is covered with dew.

The Sweetbrier rose is native to Europe and is the one we read so much about in the old garden books, in both prose and poetry. It was the favorite rose of Chaucer, Spenser, and Shakespeare. It was also the beloved rose of our earliest settlers, who brought it to this country even before the time of the Revolutionary War. The Sweetbrier is very hardy and it will grow to a height of about 10 feet, so is fine for background planting and tall hedges. However, it can be pruned and kept to any size wanted.

Two other popular briers are the so-called Austrian Brier (*Rosa foetida*) and Scotch Brier (*Rosa spinosissima*). Austrian Brier has a yellow flower and reaches about 6 feet in height, while the smaller Scotch species has double, blush-pink flowers.

MOSS ROSES

Of all rose dynasties, that of the Moss rose (*Rosa centifolia muscosa*) is the most endearing. These darlings of the nineteenth century, with their cozy Victorian appeal to our sentiments, have mostly passed from our gardens, though they still adorn chinaware, valentines, and floral prints. The graceful, nodding double blooms rising out of their charming enclosures of thick green or brownish "moss" never fail to attract admirers. In the pleasant revival of interest in the shrub and old-fashioned roses now current with enthusiasts, the moss roses happily are making a comeback.

Perhaps because mosses are redolent of a simplicity and unsophistication very telling in contrast with our modern hybrids, it was long believed that they came into Western gardens in ancient times. We now know that the old pink or common moss originated as a mutation of *Rosa centifolia* (itself probably only four hundred years old and thus a child among the roses) no earlier than the end of the seventeenth century. More than a hundred years later, however, the Age of Victoria took the Moss rose to its collective heart, and the nineteenth century was its heyday.

There are two distinct types of these plants: In the first group are the *centifolia* hybrids and mutations, marked by soft, thick, fragrant moss. Among these, the "crested moss," though not properly a Moss rose at all, is generally included. The second group includes the hybrids of the autumn or four-seasons

16

Damask, with stiff, upright growth and long, "harsh" mossing. Several of these varieties bloom again in the fall. The true Damask roses (*Rosa damascena*) have flowers that are pink to white, semi-double and double, and their fragrance is the best of *all* roses. They range from 4 to 6 feet tall.

Moss roses require a little more attention than their ancestral types. Because their mossy excrescences are sticky, they can be happy hunting grounds for aphids unless occasionally dusted; some varieties may also need mildew control. Nevertheless being sturdy shrubs, they will thrive even without such special care. Their chief cultural peculiarity is in the matter of pruning, best stated in one word: *Don't.* Cut them when they are to bloom to encourage bushiness; thin out old canes every few years, if necessary; but any cutting after September will often mean no flowers next year. The exceptions to this rule are the two or three everblooming kinds which may be pruned in December, somewhat like hybrid teas.

A remarkable number of these old favorites still flourish. A recent English book on shrub roses lists forty varieties, at least twenty of which are available from American growers. Here are some of the most rewarding:

Blanche Moreau	White
Capitaine John Ingram	Purplish-crimson
Devil de Paul Fontaine	Rosy-maroon
Nuits de Dalmas	Maroon-purple
Gloire de Mousseaux	Pink
Jeanne de Montfort	Pink
Mme Louis Leveque	Pink
Old Pink Moss	Pink
Comtesse de Murinais	White
Salet	Pink
Rose du Roi (damask)	Red
Marie Louise (damask)	Pink
Four Seasons (damask)	Pink
York and Lancaster (damask)	Pink to white
Mme Hardy (damask)	White

OTHER OLD-FASHIONED ROSES

The following are several other classes of old-fashioned roses that are worthy of mention:

Rosa alba (York Rose) is vigorous, but occasionally leggy, with semi-double white blooms and large scarlet fruits. It is a fine 6-foot accent or specimen.

17

The three widely grown varieties are Maiden's Blush, Cuisse de Nymphe Emue, and Mme Legras de St. Germain.

Rosa borboniana (Bourbon) is mostly recurrent (repeat bloom) with large, well-formed, white, pink, or red flowers, borne individually or in small clusters. They range between 4 and 7 feet tall and the best known of this group are: Souvenir de la Malmaison (pink), Boule de Neige (white), Commandant Beaurepaire (deep pink), Mme Pierre Oger (rose-pink), and La Reine Victoria (rose-pink).

Rosa centifolia (Cabbage or "Hundred-leaf Rose") has a basic pink color, with numerous hybrids of other hues. It rarely gets fruits. A few of these 6-footers will screen a compost heap or utility yard. The best known species still available are Chapeau de Napoleon, Fantin Latour, and Unique Chapeau.

Rosa gallica (French Rose) is mostly a compact shrub of upright growth, about 4 feet in height, with pink, red, purple, or striped flowers that are nonrecurrent (without repeat blooms).

Rosa noisettiana (Noisette) is basically a Southern rose but a few hardy ones—Mme Alfred Carriere, Gloire de Dijon, and William Allen Richardson—have been grown in the North. The medium-sized, semi-double, blush-pink blossoms, sometimes a hundred in a cluster, are borne at the ends of canes. Outstanding varieties include Lamarque, Marechal Niel, Reve d'Or, and Solfaterre.

In most cases, these and other previously mentioned roses in this group—hybrid perpetuals, China roses, tea roses, hybrid musks, sweetbrier, and moss roses—are of sentimental interest to collectors but are generally inferior to our so-called "modern" roses. However, in recent years, many rose fanciers are collecting and making them a part of their rose gardens. Most of the noteworthy varieties mentioned in this book are obtainable—but not always with ease—from the few nurseries in the United States that specialize in old-fashioned roses.

Shrub Roses

Shrub roses are actually a miscellaneous group of wild species, hybrids, and varieties that develop an open-bush type of growth that is useful in general landscape work. They are hardy in all sections of the country. While their

18

Figure 5 Popular shrub roses: *(top-left) Rosa rugosa; (top right) Rosa xanthina; (bottom-left)* Blanc Double de Coubert; *(bottom-right)* Nevada.

19

flowers do not equal in size or form those of other types of roses, many bear very attractive seed pods in the fall. They have very fine foliage and some are quite useful for hedges or screen plantings.

The following list includes the most popular varieties:

Rosa multiflora	White to red
Rosa hugonis	Yellow
Rosa moyesii	Blood red
Rosa pomifera	Pink
Rosa rubrifolia	Pink
Rosa setigera	Pink
Rosa rugosa	Purplish red
Rosa rugosa alba	White
Rosa spinossissima	White
Dr. Eckener	Coppery rose
F. J. Grootendorst	Red
Gruss an Teplitz	Red
Harison's Yellow	Deep yellow
Nevada	White
Sir Thomas Lipton	White
Pink Grootendorst	Pink
Sarah Van Fleet	Pink
Frau Dagmar Hartopp	Pink
Nymphenburg	Pink
Lady Curzon	Pink
Bonn	Coral-scarlet
Max Graf	Pink
Autumn Bouquet	Pink
Flamingo	Pink
Constance Spry	Pink
Rugosa Magnifica	Carmine
Skyrocket	Red
Ruskin	Red
Lipstick	Cerise
Blanc Double de Coubert	White
Patricia Macoun	White
Sea Foam	White
The Fairy	Pink

Tree or Standard Roses

This class refers to the form of the plant rather than to the type of flower. Any bush type of rose—usually the hybrid teas, hybrid perpetual, and floribunda varieties—can be made into a tree form, and many of the better known varieties are now available as tree roses. They are made by grafting other roses, usually with good flower size, color, and form, onto a special understock. As trees, they make interesting additions to the large formal garden. In smaller gardens, they must be used with care, perhaps as specimen shrubs rather than strictly as roses.

The following list includes the most popular varieties:

Angel Face	Lavender
Charlotte Armstrong	Red
Chrysler Imperial	Red
First Prize	Pink
Mister Lincoln	Red
Pascali	White
Peace	Cream-pink
Portrait	Pink
Queen Elizabeth	Pink
Sea Foam	White
Summer Sunshine	Yellow
The Fairy	Pink
Tropicana	Orange-red

The plants are subject to winter injury. In sections where the winters are severe, they need special protection (see page 133).

CLIMBING ROSES

Climbing roses include all varieties that produce long cane growth and require some sort of support to hold the plants up off the ground. They are often trained on fences or trellises, and some are used to cover banks and aid in holding the soil in place. Climbing roses are rather hardy.

Figure 6 Two uses of the climbing class of roses.

Climbing roses may be used to relieve the plainness of a bare wall, partially conceal an unattractive view, or serve as a hedge or fence and, if planted closely, have winter value as a snow fence. If given adequate support, climbing roses will make a satisfactory barrier and, with the present high cost of lumber, can be wisely substituted for an all-wood fence. If proper varieties are selected, the roses will outlast most conventional fences.

When trained on posts, the pillar-type roses relieve the monotony of formal gardens by adding height and, for this purpose, they are most satisfactory and less expensive than tree roses.

Climbing roses, like bush roses, are grouped into several classes. There is much overlapping among classes, and some varieties could qualify under several. The following classes are now generally used in most catalogs: ramblers, large-flowered climbers, everblooming climbers, climbing hybrid teas, climbing poly-anthas, climbing floribundas, and pillar roses. Unfortunately, it is often difficult

22

to decide just where one class ends and another begins. But remember that some climbing roses are particularly valuable for covering walls or fences . . . others for forming a rambling mass of rose beauty, and some are ideal subjects for training on posts. Few, if any, are adaptable for all of these purposes and many are definitely unsuited for more than one.

Ramblers

Rambler roses are very rapid growers. They sometimes develop canes as long as 20 feet in one season. The flowers are small, less than 2 inches across, and are borne in dense clusters. The plants flower only once during a season and on wood that was produced the preceding year. The foliage is glossy and the plants are very hardy, but, unfortunately, many varieties are very susceptible to mildew. Rambler roses are not nearly so popular as they were a few years ago. They are being replaced by other climbing types that bear larger flowers and are less subject to mildew.

Some of the better varieties are:

Bloomfield Courage	Red
Crimson Rambler	Red
Excelsa	Red
Hiawatha	Red with white eye
Dorothy Perkins	Pink to white
White Dorothy	White
Chevy Chase	Red
Evangeline	Rosy-white
Sanders' White Rambler	White
Minnehaha	Pink
Aviateur Bleriot	Yellow
Brownell's Rambler	Yellow

Large-Flowered Climbers

Large-flowered climbers grow rather slowly in comparison with ramblers. They are often trained on posts or some other type of small support, and may require rather heavy annual pruning to keep them in bounds. These roses are well

23

Figure 7   The large-flowered climber, Paul's Scarlet.

adapted to small gardens where they may be trained against a wall, fence, or small trellis. When the plants are grown well, the flowers are rather large and useful for cutting. Many varieties do not bloom so freely when the canes are trained vertically rather than horizontally.

24

Plate 1   Command Performance, hybrid tea

Plate 2   White Knight, hybrid tea (left)
Golden Prince, hybrid tea (above)

Plate 3   Camelot, grandiflora (top)
Mister Lincoln, hybrid tea (above)

Plate 4   Chrysler Imperial, hybrid tea (above)
           Lady Elgin, hybrid tea (right)

Plate 5   Peace, hybrid tea

Plate 6   Queen Elizabeth, grandiflora (left)
Aquarius, grandiflora (below)
Taj Mahal, hybrid tea (bottom)

Plate 7   Scarlet Knight, grandiflora (right)
             Red Gold, floribunda (below)
             Fashion, floribunda (bottom right)

Plate 8   Fire King, floribunda (right)
           Sonoma, floribunda (below)
           Rhonda, everblooming climber (bottom right)

From among the varieties available, the following are recommended:

Bess Lovett .... Red
Dr. Huey .... Red-maroon
Paul's Scarlet Climber .... Red
Dr. W. Van Fleet .... Pink
Mary Wallace .... Pink
City of York .... White
Mary Lovett .... White
Silver Moon .... White
Doubloons .... Yellow
Belle of Portugal .... Yellow
Gardenia .... Yellow
Glenn Dale .... White
Jacotte .... Salmon and apricot

Everblooming Climbers

The everblooming climbers are not so strong-growing or continuous in bloom-ing as the hybrid teas. They produce an abundance of flowers in the early summer. This is followed with a few scattered blooms until fall when, if grow-ing conditions are good, they may again bear rather heavily. Plant breeders are improving this class of rose rather rapidly. Eventually, climbers will be available that will be as continuous in blooming as hybrid teas and will also be more winter-hardy.

Of the varieties available, the following are very satisfactory:

Red Empress .... Red
Blaze .... Red
Flash .... Red
Don Juan .... Red
Pillar of Fire .... Coral-red
Dr. J. H. Nicolas .... Pink
New Dawn .... Pink
Aloha .... Pink
Blossomtime .... Pink
Claire Martin .... Pink
Coral Dawn .... Coral-pink
Gold Rush .... Yellow
Golden Showers .... Yellow

Mermaid .... Yellow and orange
Mrs. Whitman Cross .... Yellow and orange
Penelope .... White
White Dawn .... White

Climbing Hybrid Teas

Climbing hybrid tea roses have originated as seedlings and as chance sports of bush varieties. When a bush hybrid tea produces a cane that has the climbing character, the new type of plant is usually given the same name as the bush variety from which it originated—for instance, Climbing Peace. The climbing forms of hybrid teas, in general, do not have so pronounced a continuous blooming habit as their parents. The flowers, foliage, and other characters, however, are usually identical. The climbing hybrid teas are just as susceptible to winter injury as the bush forms, and require good winter protection in Northern areas.

Among the best climbing hybrid tea varieties available are the following:

Climbing Crimson Glory .... Red
Climbing Christopher Stone .... Red
Climbing Golden Dawn .... Yellow
Climbing Mrs. Sam McGredy .... Blend
Climbing Talisman .... Pink
Climbing Picture .... Pink
Climbing Cecile Brunner .... Pink
Climbing Santa Anita .... Pink
Climbing Etoile de Hollande .... Red
Climbing Charlotte Armstrong .... Red
Climbing Peace .... Blend
Climbing Mme Henri Guillot .... Blend

Climbing Floribundas and Polyanthas

These types, like the climbing hybrid teas, have originated as sports and seed-lings from polyanthas and floribundas. Their flowers are generally identical with the bush forms from which they originated, and they also are fairly con-tinuous in blooming. They are hardier than the climbing hybrid teas, but not hardy enough to be grown in severe winter climates, unless provided with winter protection.

Some of the better varieties are:

Climbing Goldilocks .... Yellow
Climbing Pinocchio .... Pink blend
Climbing Pinkie .... Pink
Climbing Summer Snow .... White

Creeping or Trailing Roses

The creeping or trailing roses are actually climbing roses whose canes are sufficiently pliable to enable them to lie close to the ground. They may be trained as climbers but bloom best when grown in a prostrate position on banks, hillsides, or waste places. If the soil has been well enriched before planting, the growth will develop into a dense and exceedingly attractive mat which will not only discourage trespassers and weeds but, to a great extent, will also prevent erosion. Weed control and erosion are minimized if the ground is heavily mulched with straw until the plants are well established.

Some of the better varieties are:

Rosa laevigata .... White
Rosa wichuraiana .... Pink
Max Graf .... Pink
Lady Duncan .... Pink
Little Compton Creeper .... Rose-pink
Red Cherokee .... Red
Coral Creeper .... Apricot and pink
Golden Glow .... Yellow
Carpet of Gold .... Yellow
Baltimore Belle .... White
White Banksia .... White

Pillar Roses

A pillar rose is an intermediate type—somewhere between the climber and the bush rose. Often it is described as a very long-caned, bush type that grows to

8 feet or more. It is not sufficiently vigorous to be recognized as a climber and has wood that is too short and rigid to ramble. This class of rose is generally trained against a pillar or post and is employed on lamp posts, along porches, or mixed in with other plants for a spectacular display of concentrated color. Pillar roses as a class are fairly hardy, but they require heavy pruning of laterals (see page 130) to keep in pillar form.

A few of the better varieties are:

High Noon .... Yellow
Paul's Lemon Pillar .... Yellow
Clytemnestra .... Yellow
Morning Stars .... White
Prosperity .... White
Reichsprasident von Hindenburg .... Pink
Don Juan .... Red
Gladiator .... Rose-red
Pillar of Fire .... Red

MINIATURE ROSES

Called the jewels of the rose world, the miniatures are exquisitely formed replicas of the hybrid tea rose, but on an almost incredibly small scale. Long buds no longer than a grain of wheat, or round ones smaller than a pea, are perfect in every detail. As many as seventy little petals can be counted in a double miniature rose. These blossoms measure only ¾ to 1½ inches across. The bushes, too, are small, measuring from 6 to 12 inches in height, depending on the variety, with little leaves, stems, and even thorns—all in perfect scale.

Miniature roses, though finely wrought, are rugged and bear a generous number of flowers. Furthermore, they are hardy and, given care, will last for years. The little roses may be grown outdoors in rock gardens or as an edge for small pools or walks. They are especially good as edging for borders of larger roses, but for this use they must be carefully placed. The small bushes should be set far enough forward so as not to be shaded and overhung; also, they should not be close enough to the larger roses to be robbed of moisture and nutrients. Miniature roses may also be grown indoors (see page 140).

There are three types of the hybrid dwarf roses: stocky miniatures, 6 to

29

Figure 8 Coral Dawn is a good pillar rose.

12 inches in height; larger, heavier-stemmed, and heavier-leaved varieties show-ing their polyantha ancestry; and the more recently developed climbing minia-tures, sprawling sometimes 5 feet wide and high. With these might be included the tree-rose type, miniature scions grafted on stems and roots of larger roses. The dwarf roses are nearly always grown on their own roots.

Figure 9 The popular polyantha rose, the Fairy, is shown both as a bush rose and as a tree or standard rose.

Miniatures come in most of the colors found in larger roses—white through cream, shell pink to deep rose, and all shades of red to crimson-black. There are also lavenders, magentas, yellows from cream to butter, and several bicolors. New varieties are appearing every year. Among the better varieties are the following:

Shrubs, 6 inches or taller

Scarlet Gem	Orange-scarlet
Baby Gold Star	Yellow
Midget	Red
Oakington Ruby	Red
Pixie Rose	Pale pink
Rosa rouletti	Pink
Sweet Fairy	Pink
Tom Thumb	Red
Pompon de Paris	Pink
Bo-Peep	Rose-pink
Frosty	White
Bit O' Sunshine	Yellow
Jackie	Yellow
Cinderella	White
Dwarfking	Red
Centennial Miss	Red
Red Imp	Red
Baby Darling	Apricot
Starina	Orange-red
Chipper	Coral-pink
Shooting Star	Yellow-red

Climbers, 3 to 5 feet tall

Red Wand	Red
Hi-Ho	Light red
Climbing Jackie	Yellow
Little Showoff	Yellow
Pink Cameo	Rose-pink

Tree, 10 to 15 inches tall

Dian	Red
Mona Ruth	Red
Cinderella	White
Baby Gold Star	Yellow

31

Figure 10   The rose, Pixie, both as a miniature bush and as a tree. Note comparison of size with a woman's garden glove.

FRAGRANCE IN ROSES

Fragrance, to many people, is the very soul of the rose. True, no other garden flower has ever had so much to offer in color, form, and variety; still, rose lovers of every generation have held fragrance to be its outstanding virtue. "The rose looks fair," wrote Shakespeare, "but fairer we it deem for that sweet odor doth in it live."

32

There is considerable controversy, however, as to whether modern roses are as fragrant as their ancestors. It is true that hybridists have inevitably sacrificed odor to beauty of color in creating some of the exquisite new varieties. Nevertheless, many modern roses preserve the old enchanting perfumes while others have a sweetness all their own. And the trend is certainly to breed scents back into the lovely modern creations, as will be noted by anyone familiar with the new introductions. Given two roses of equal quality, the one fragrant and the other not, the gardener will choose to plant the sweet-smelling variety.

Rose fragrance is usually based on several distinct types, with others amounting to blends. Before the advent of the hybrid perpetuals, the four basic scents were those of the teas, the damasks, the *gallicas*, and the *centifolias*. The faint fragrance of China roses combined with the heavy perfume of *Rosa gallica* gave us the deliciously scented hybrid perpetuals. In turn, these were crossed with the tea roses to produce the hybrid teas, some of which are intensely fragrant while others are practically scentless.

Some rose fanciers hold that no two varieties of roses develop precisely the same scent and that individual blossoms on one plant may differ somewhat. The latter assumption is probably a matter of degree rather than of actual difference, and is related to atmospheric conditions and to the age of flowers.

Figure 11 Two roses—*(left)* hybrid tea, Chrysler Imperial, and climber, Don Juan—that combine beauty and fragrance.

Fragrance in roses is most pronounced just as the blossom opens and weakens as the bloom ages. It arises from the presence of a volatile oil that appears most abundantly in the cells near the base and on the undersides of the petals. This oil does not accumulate or take the form of drops but is given off by exhalation almost as soon as it is generated. Formation and dispersion are most rapid on a warm, moist day.

Usually about one ton of freshly picked petals is required to produce a pound of attar of roses, but the amount of oil obtained varies considerably from season to season. The varieties used chiefly in the production of this essence are natural hybrids of *centifolia* and *gallica*. When quality is desirable, the former predominate, while the latter supply quantity.

Roses and perfume are closely associated in our minds, but we should not forget the lovely varieties without fragrance. Among the moderns, some strikingly beautiful specimens are scentless. The new variety Peace apparently has everything to be desired in a rose except this one quality. Frau Karl Druschki, the most beautiful of all white roses, is another that lacks perfume and, popular as it is among rose growers, it would be even more greatly prized if it were scented.

Happily, the plant breeder, having achieved the ultimate in color, is now making a sincere effort to endow new hybrids with fragrance. Here is a list of the more highly fragrant of the modern roses:

Crimson Glory	Etoile de Hollande	Angel Face
Sutter's Gold	Mme Jules Bouch	La Canadiene
Tiffany	Polly	Mister Lincoln
Royal Highness	Imperial Potentate	Eiffel Tower
Flying Cloud	Shot Silk	Capistrano
Tropicana	Texas Centennial	Tawny Gold
Granada	Oklahoma	Golden Dawn
Iceberg	Don Juan	Neige Parfum
Spartan	Chrysler Imperial	Hector Deane
Apricot Nectar	Mirandy	Christopher Stone
Polynesian Sunset	Suzan Lotthe	Girona
Orchid Masterpiece	The Doctor	Heart's Desire
President Herbert Hoover	Kordes Perfecta	Angel's Maten
Tallyho	Miss All-America Beauty	Charles Mallerin
Radiance	Fashion	Sweet Afton
Miss Clipper	Ma Perkins	Blossomtime

2

HOW TO BUY ROSE PLANTS

"A rose, is a rose, is a rose and that is all you can say about a rose" may satisfy a poet, but a home gardener confronted with making a selection from a rose catalog or even a nursery will find that it is not quite that simple. Before going into details on purchasing roses, we should like to make two points.

First, the best way to get off to a good start with roses is to select the best varieties. Vigor, productivity, and disease resistance are particularly important to the beginner, for sucess or failure can make you a rabid rose fan or forever discourage you from having a rose garden.

Second, where should you buy roses—from a reliable nurseryman and garden store or by catalog? There are many reliable producers of rose plants vitally interested in your success. But be on guard against those few whose only consideration is your first order. They are compelled to unload their inferior products at reduced prices through various outlets.

Rose "bargains" usually result either in dissatisfaction or complete failure. They are of inferior stock that has been improperly graded, mislabeled, and poorly handled. The superior product of the conscientious nurseryman may seem high-priced in comparison but he gives you good dollar-value in properly graded and clearly labeled plants. From these you get more ultimate satisfaction than from the ten-dollar-a-dozen department-store collections that are available in many towns each spring. You will find that the reliable nurseryman often lists collections of popular and mass-produced varieties that represent exceptionally good values for the beginner at moderate prices.

When purchasing roses, keep in mind that you are investing in a plant that should serve you well for many years. Therefore, take your time in making your selections and spend the little extra money sometimes required to purchase the best rose stock. You will be well repaid over the years.

WAYS OF BUYING ROSES

Roses are sold in two basic forms: bare-root dormant bushes and plants in containers.

DORMANT ROSES

Dormant packaged roses are sold generally without soil about the roots by mail-order nurseries and garden stores in early spring and late fall. Those for sale in spring are dug from the fields in late fall, while those purchased in fall are just as they are lifted from the field. In the latter case, they are almost certain to be good live plants. When properly stored over the winter and sold the following spring before they have started to sprout, they will keep alive and be just as good a buy as they were the previous fall. However, if the growers or dealers do not have the necessary storage facilities, the bushes may be permitted to dehydrate to a point where they become severely weakened or even dead when sold.

To prevent dehydration during storage, some commercial growers wax the tops of the plants. The wax, however, sometimes results in injury to the plant if it is applied in too hot a condition. This damage is difficult to detect, and subsequently the rose dies. Because of this, in recent years many growers have been using protective coverings of plastic or polyethylene in place of wax. While we are not condemning waxing in general, we find that most rosarians prefer dormant roses in plastic coverings.

When purchasing dormant roses, choose plants that have plump, green canes with smooth, unshriveled bark, and a good, well balanced root system.

36

Figure 12 Most roses are shipped dormant with their roots packed in sphagnum moss.

The roots should be moist and fresh and should have protection from drying out. A bush in good condition will have weight; dried out bushes will be abnormally light and brittle.

In recent years, so-called pre-planted dormant roses have been made available to rose lovers by some growers. While the plants are dormant, the roots are encased in a good soil mixture and wrapped in a material that will disintegrate in the ground after planting. This gives the rose a longer, safer shelf-life and certainly makes it much easier to plant.

37

Figure 13   Potted roses can be planted even when they are in flower.

ROSES IN CONTAINERS

Many commercial growers are planting their roses in plastic, metal, or tarpaper containers of 2- to 5-gallon capacity. Such potted roses offer an excellent means of selecting plants in bud or bloom, even in summer. Because plants are potted in soil, transplanting does not disturb the roots. (Remember, however, the container must be removed before planting.) Another great advantage: It is easy to arrange color when plants are in flower.

Unfortunately, container-planted roses cannot be shipped by parcel post. They are bulky and heavy and, consequently, are expensive to crate and ship by any means. For this reason, most dealers will not ship container-stocks.

38

ROSE GRADING SYSTEM

To purchase roses wisely, you should know the various grades of plants. These standards were set by the American Rose Society and the American Association of Nurserymen. All reputable growers adhere to them. The grades are defined as follows:

For Tea, Hybrid Tea, Grandiflora, Hybrid Perpetual, and Miscellaneous Bush Roses: #1 grade—roses in this grade must have three or more strong canes, two of which must be 18 inches or more in length before cutting by the seller, with the exception of some of the light-growing varieties, which are to have three canes (or more), two of which are to be 16 inches and up, one cane to be 18 inches, branched not more than 3 inches above the bud union. #1½ grade—roses in this grade must have two or more strong canes that are 15 inches or more in length with the exception of some of the light-growing varieties, which must have two strong canes 13 inches and up, and branched not higher than 3 inches above the bud union. #2 grade—roses in this grade must have two or more strong canes 12 inches and up, with the exception of light-growing varieties, which must have two canes 10 inches and up.

For Floribunda Roses: #1 grade—roses in this grade must have three or more strong canes, two of which are 15 inches or more in length, with the exception of light-growing varieties which must have three canes 13 inches and up, branched not more than 3 inches above the bud union. #1½ grade —roses in this grade must have two or more strong canes that are 14 inches or more in length (lighter varieties, 12 inches or more in length) and must originate not more than 3 inches above the bud graft union. #2 grade— no value.

For Polyantha Roses and light-growing Floribunda Roses: #1 grade—roses in this grade must have four or more canes that are 12 inches or more in length and must originate not more than 3 inches above the bud graft union. #1½ grade—roses in this grade must have three or more canes that are 10 inches or more in length and must originate not more than 3 inches above the bud graft union. #2 grade—no value.

For Climbing Roses: #1 grade—roses in this grade must have three or more strong canes that are 24 inches or more in length and must originate not more than 3 inches above the bud graft union. #1½ grade—roses in this grade must have two or more strong canes that are 18 inches or more in length and must originate not more than 3 inches above the bud graft union. It is wise to select only #1 or 1½ grade, either of which will develop into a good plant. #2 plants start out with a handicap that they often cannot overcome. Plants should be two-year-old, field-grown stock in dormant stage, but in fresh condition, root and top.

Often the nurseryman will have cut all the canes back to 12 or 14 inches and will have trimmed back the roots. This reduces the shipping cost by permitting the plants to be sent in smaller cartons. If the cut-back canes and roots are of good quality and caliber and the root development well balanced, these bushes should be accepted as #1 or 1½ grade if so labeled. The cutback has usually readied them for planting. Incidentally, the grading system can be used as a guide when purchasing roses, but remember that most reputable growers are more generous in grading of their plants than they are required to be.

PATENTS VS. NON-PATENTS

A tag on a rose plant usually indicates that it is a patented one. Actually, the initials P.A.F. stand for Patent Applied For. This means that the hybridizer or introducer has applied for a plant patent so that he can control the propagating rights on a variety for a specified length of time. When the patent is granted he is assured of a greater return on his investment for the development of the rose. Once a patent is granted, a number will be assigned to the variety and will be so indicated after the variety name—PP 2540, for example. During the time the patent remains active the rose plant generally sells for slightly more than a nonpatented variety or one on which the patent has expired.

It is important to remember that a patent tag is no guarantee of a rose's superiority. True, many roses are excellent, proven varieties. But some patented roses have proven to be unsatisfactory under certain growing conditions. Some of the finest roses do not carry the small metal patent tag.

OTHER AIDS FOR THE ROSARIAN

The changing pageant of the catalogs that come out every year, the recommendations of the All-America Rose Selections, the American Rose Society, and similar agencies, and garden publications are the most effective sources of current information for the average rose gardener.

Catalogs, particularly from rose specialists, are a great help in selecting roses. Besides color descriptions, you will find general comment on growth and blooming habits, presence or absence of fragrance, and any special awards the variety may have been given.

ALL-AMERICA ROSE SELECTIONS

A metal tag with the initials AARS indicates that that rose was an All-America Selection. This award is given to outstanding roses by a non-profit organization that was set up for the specific purpose of testing new varieties of roses to determine which, if any, are worthy of recommendation to the buying public as the best of the new introductions. The awards were first given in 1940.

For a rose to be so nominated, it must first be planted in the twenty-two testing stations located throughout the United States where the conditions of soil and climate are representative of all the areas where roses are generally grown. During the two-year trial period, the roses are carefully observed and their various characteristics rated by official All-America Rose Selection judges who have had wide experience in growing and scoring roses. The judges score the roses on a numerical system set up by the Scoring Schedule Committee. Here are the qualities sought in All-America roses:

1. NOVELTY—An outstanding quality that sets the variety apart as different from roses already in the trade.
2. VIGOR—Healthy, consistent growth and endurance through heat and cold.
3. HABIT—Orderliness, grace, and uniform plant-shape.
4. DISEASE RESISTANCE—Ability to resist blackspot, mildew, rust, and other rose diseases.

41

5. FOLIAGE—Color, texture, form, size, and abundance.

6. BUD FORM—Quality, size, shape, and beauty of buds.

7. FLORIFEROUSNESS—Abundance of healthy blossoms throughout the season.

8. FLOWER FORM—Consistent shape, size, and beauty of flowers.

9. SUBSTANCE—Texture and endurance of petals.

10. COLOR OPENING—Color value and harmony of new flowers.

11. COLOR FINISHING—Beauty of mature flower-color, grace while aging.

12. FRAGRANCE—Strength and desirability of scent.

13. STEM—Length, sturdiness, and ability to support bloom.

The highest-scoring roses are announced each year. Winning plants bear the official green and white oval metal seal bearing the AARS symbol and the words, "This AARS rose, after two years of actual growing tests in all parts of the United States, has proved to be a superior variety." Each year in July, the winners for the following year are announced.

Figure 14 Two AARS winners over the years: *(left)* Apollo; *(right)* Fire King.

42

ALL-AMERICA ROSE SELECTIONS

Year	Award Winner	Color	Class
1973	Gypsy	Orange-red	Hybrid Tea
	Medallion	Apricot-buff	Hybrid Tea
	Electron	Rose-pink	Hybrid Tea
1972	Apollo	Yellow	Hybrid Tea
	Portrait	White edge on pink	Hybrid Tea
1971	Aquarius	Pink blend	Grandiflora
	Command Performance	Orange-red	Hybrid Tea
	Redgold	Red edge on yellow	Floribunda
1970	First Prize	Rose-red	Hybrid Tea
1969	Angel Face	Lavender	Floribunda
	Comanche	Scarlet-orange	Grandiflora
	Gene Boerner	Pink	Floribunda
	Pascali	White	Hybrid Tea
1968	Europeana	Red	Floribunda
	Miss All-American Beauty	Pink	Hybrid Tea
	Scarlet Knight	Scarlet-red	Grandiflora
1967	Bewitched	Clear, phlox pink	Hybrid Tea
	Gay Princess	Shell pink	Floribunda
	Lucky Lady	Creamy, shrimp pink	Grandiflora
	Roman Holiday	Orange-red	Floribunda
1966	American Heritage	Ivory tinged carmine	Hybrid Tea
	Apricot Nectar	Apricot	Floribunda
	Matterhorn	White	Hybrid Tea
1965	Camelot	Shrimp pink	Grandiflora
	Mister Lincoln	Deep red	Hybrid Tea
1964	Granada	Red and yellow	Hybrid Tea
	Saratoga	White	Floribunda
1963	Royal Highness	Light pink	Hybrid Tea
	Tropicana	Orange-red	Hybrid Tea
1962	Christian Dior	Bright crimson	Hybrid Tea
	Golden Slippers	Gold and orange	Floribunda
	John S. Armstrong	Dark red	Grandiflora
	King's Ransom	Chrome yellow	Hybrid Tea

Year	Award Winner	Color	Class
1961	Duet	Pink bicolor	Hybrid Tea
	Pink Parfait	Light pink	Grandiflora
1960	Garden Party	White tinged with pink	Hybrid Tea
	Fire King	Vermilion	Floribunda
	Saraband	Scarlet-orange	Floribunda
1959	Starfire	Cherry red	Grandiflora
	Ivory Fashion	Ivory white	Floribunda
1958	Fusillier	Orange-red	Floribunda
	Gold Cup	Yellow	Floribunda
	White Knight	White	Hybrid Tea
1957	Golden Showers	Yellow	Climber
	White Bouquet	White	Floribunda
1956	Circus	Multicolor	Floribunda
1955	Tiffany	Bicolor; yellow, pink	Hybrid Tea
	Jiminy Cricket	Coral-orange	Floribunda
	Queen Elizabeth	Delicate pink	Grandiflora
1954	Lilibet	Clear pink	Floribunda
	Mojave	Apricot-orange	Hybrid Tea
1953	Chrysler Imperial	Crimson	Hybrid Tea
	Ma Perkins	Coral shell pink	Floribunda
1952	Fred Howard	Yellow, penciled pink	Hybrid Tea
	Vogue	Cherry coral	Floribunda
	Helen Traubel	Apricot-pink	Hybrid Tea
1950	Fashion	Coral-pink	Floribunda
	Mission Bells	Salmon	Hybrid Tea
	Capistrano	Pink	Hybrid Tea
	Sutter's Gold	Golden yellow	Hybrid Tea
1949	Forty-Niner	Bicolor; red, yellow	Hybrid Tea
	Tallyho	Two-tone pink	Hybrid Tea
1948	Diamond Jubilee	Buff	Hybrid Tea
	High Noon*	Yellow	Climber
	Nocturne	Dark red	Hybrid Tea
	Pinkie	Light rose-pink	Polyantha
	San Fernando	Currant red	Hybrid Tea
	Taffeta	Two-tone pink-yellow	Hybrid Tea

Year	Award Winner	Color	Class
1947	Rubaiyat	Cerise	Hybrid Tea
1946	Peace	Pale gold	Hybrid Tea
1945	Floradora	Salmon-rose	Floribunda
	Horace McFarland	Buff pink	Hybrid Tea
	Mirandy	Crimson	Hybrid Tea
1944	Fred Edmunds*	Apricot	Hybrid Tea
	Katherine T. Marshall	Deep pink	Hybrid Tea
	Lowell Thomas	Butter yellow	Hybrid Tea
	Mme Chiang Kai-shek	Light yellow	Hybrid Tea
	Mme Marie Curie	Golden yellow	Hybrid Tea
1943	Grande Duchess Charlotte	Wine red	Hybrid Tea
	Mary Margaret McBride	Rose-pink	Hybrid Tea
1942	Heart's Desire	Deep rose-red	Hybrid Tea
1941	Charlotte Armstrong	Cerise	Hybrid Tea
	Apricot Queen	Apricot	Hybrid Tea
	California	Golden yellow	Hybrid Tea
1940	Dickson's Red	Scarlet	Hybrid Tea
	Flash	Oriental red	Climber
	The Chief	Salmon-red	Hybrid Tea
	World's Fair	Deep red	Floribunda

When buying any of the All-America roses in local nurseries, look for the famous green-and-white tag that is attached to all winners. This tag gives the variety name and carries the symbol of a rose surrounded by the initials AARS. Garden catalogs always indicate the AARS winners.

AMERICAN ROSE SOCIETY RATING

Another good check on the quality of rose plants you plan to purchase is the American Rose Society ratings. This well-known society (see page 47) publishes an annual buying guide based on accumulated reports from hundreds of members in this country and Canada. Hybrid tea, floribunda, grandiflora, and

* Denotes sectional recommendation.

climber classes are rated on a scale of 10. A national rating of 10 is a perfect rose (none has made it yet); from 9 to 9.9 are outstanding varieties; from 8 to 8.9 are excellent roses; from 7 to 7.9 are good; and from 6 to 6.9 are fair. Any ratings lower than 6 represent varieties of questionable value. The following is a listing of some highly rated hybrid teas and floribundas.

HYBRID TEAS

Red	Points	*Pink (cont.)*	Points
Chrysler Imperial	8.9	Carla	8.0
Tropicana	8.8	First Love	8.0
Fragrant Cloud	8.6	Sabine	7.9
Mister Lincoln	8.5	Bel Ange	7.9
Charlotte Armstrong	8.4	Prima Ballerina	7.9
Crimson Glory	8.3	South Seas	7.9
Big Ben	8.2	Uncle Sam	7.9
Avon	8.0	*White*	
Oriental Charm	8.0	Pascali	8.3
Proud Land	8.0	Garden Party	7.9
Red Devil	8.0	Jacques Carteau	7.7
Oklahoma	7.9	Sweet Afton	7.7
George Dickson	7.9	Burnaby	7.6
Otto Miller	7.8	Matterhorn	7.5
Pharaoh	7.8	Dresden	7.5
Yellow		Innocence	7.5
King's Ransom	7.8	*Blends*	
Gold Glow	7.6	Peace	9.4
Lemon Spice	7.6	Tiffany	9.1
Summer Sunshine	7.6	Confidence	8.4
First Federal Gold	7.6	Manuel Pinto de'Azevedo	8.4
Eclipse	7.5	Swarthmore	8.4
McGredy's Yellow	7.5	Chicago Peace	8.4
Pink		Mediterianea	8.4
First Prize	9.0	Helen Traubel	8.3
Miss All-American	8.6	Isabel de Ortiz	8.2
Royal Highness	8.6	American Heritage	7.9
Pink Favorite	8.5	Bon Voyage	7.9
Dainty Bess	8.3	Michele Meilland	7.9
Showtime	8.3	Sutter's Gold	7.8
Rubaiyat	8.2	Lucky Piece	7.8

46

FLORIBUNDAS

Red	Points	Pink	Points
Spartan	8.4	Betty Prior	9.0
Europeana	8.4	Gene Boerner	8.3
Orangeade	8.4	Tom Tom	8.2
Orange Sensation	8.3	Pink Rosette	8.1
Pied Piper	8.2	Rosenelfe	7.9
Frensham	8.2	Else Poulsen	7.8
Ginger	8.2	Pink Bountiful	7.8
Feurio	8.0	Betsy McCall	7.7
Sarabande	7.9	Rose of Tralee	7.7
Red Pinocchio	7.9	*Blends*	
Permanent Wave	7.9	Little Darling	8.6
Yellow		Dearest	8.6
Yellow Cushion	7.5	Sea Pearl	8.5
Sunbonnet	7.4	Cupid's Charm	8.4
Starlet	7.4	Border Gem	8.4
Allgold	7.4	Winifred Coulter	8.3
Arthur Bell	7.3	Vogue	8.2
White		Fashion	8.0
Iceberg	8.7	Circus	8.0
Ivory Fashion	8.0	Daily Sketch	7.9
Ice White	8.0	Violet Carson	7.9
Saratoga	7.7		
Summer Snow	7.7		
Corsage	7.5		
Shasta	7.5		

For the complete listing of modern roses and their ratings, revised annually, you can write to the American Rose Society, 4048 Roselea Place, Columbus, Ohio 43214. In addition to ratings, the listing indicates color of each rose, relative fragrance, and relative height.

ROSES AND THE CLIMATIC PROBLEM

"But can I grow roses where I live? Isn't it difficult in my section?" These questions are often asked, and the answer is simple. If you follow the general rules, including gardening practices, you can grow roses in any area of the United States.

IN THE NORTH

Any rose with a tea rose in its parentage is a challenge in the cold North, and all roses with a repeat-blooming habit have some tea in their parentage. While floribundas have much tea rose in their make-up, the floribunda varieties, Pinocchio, Vogue, or Goldilocks, are quite winter-hardy, and their flowers resemble small hybrid teas. They may kill back some but often they survive Northern winters without mound covering. They are a joy to the amateur who is not ready to provide the soil-in-wheelbarrow winter protection that hybrid teas require. The grandifloras, which have a high percentage of tea rose ancestry, should also be given hybrid-tea winter covering. See Chapter 8 for full details on fall and winter care of roses.

All Northern gardeners should try some of the "sub-zero" hybrid teas of the Brownells, in parentage half *Rose wichuraiana*. They are large bushes which, even unprotected, rarely kill back to the ground. For covering a trellis or arbor, ramblers are the only truly winter-hardy selection. They have small flowers and bloom but once. The large-flowered climbers of one-time bloom are usually hardy in most winters, especially if planted against a protective wall, but those with repeat bloom, except for New Dawn, are half tea rose in their make-up and unless taken down and covered on the ground will, during some winters, kill back severely.

Some of the more popular Brownell sub-zero hybrid teas are:

Queen o' the Lakes ....Red
Red Duchess ....Red

48

Cedric Adams ....Scarlet
Henry Field ....Rose-red
Anne Vanderbilt ....Two-tone red
Country Doctor ....Pink
Curly Pink ....Pink
Dolly Darling ....Rose-pink
King Boreas ....Yellow
V for Victory ....Yellow
Lily Pons ....White

IN THE SOUTHWEST

If you grow roses in the arid Southwest, irrigation must be practiced. There are some sections, such as from Laredo to Brownsville along the Rio Grande or in the Salt River area of Arizona near Phoenix, where flowers can be had almost the entire year. In these areas the period of frost-danger is seldom more than a few days to a month each year, and the planting of roses is preferred during this so-called winter period.

In other sections of the arid Southwest (for example in Amarillo, Albuquerque, and similar places where the January average temperature is 32 to 35 degrees and temperatures below zero are expected each year), planting is delayed until February or early March. Even in these areas, particularly choice, colorful, and fragrant blooms do develop in the cooler months of the growing season. In both the warm and the cold sections of the arid Southwest, the occurrence of blackspot is practically unknown.

Sunlight is readily available in most of the area, and roses will tolerate full sun if they are not crowded close to the south side of a building. They will also succeed if the beds are located to receive as little as six hours of sunlight a day. A planting site that is partially shaded in the afternoon is very desirable, especially if it also affords some protection from the wind, which can be as damaging to the blooms and foliage as a scarcity of water.

The selection of varieties depends on local conditions and what you expect from a rose. Plants in warm climates produce small flowers with fewer petals and less color intensity than the same varieties in cool climates. Many gardeners in warm climates are satisfied with the flowers of Briarcliff, Talisman, or Snow

Gnu, knowing that the flower-quality becomes better with the arrival of cool weather.

If extreme hardiness and little care is your aim in selecting roses, your planting might consist of climbers such as Paul's Scarlet, with its tremendous display in early spring, or Blaze, which blooms recurrently. Also try the pure white hybrid perpetual, Frau Karl Druschki, which is hardy and has its main production of blooms just in the spring, or species such as Austrian Copper, Harison's Yellow, or Hugo Rose.

Figure 15 When several plants of one variety are grouped together, they are very effective. The plants shown here are floribun

Climbers such as Mermaid and the Banksia roses withstand blackspot infection but cannot endure hard freezes. The common Radiance varieties (Radiance, Red Radiance, and Mrs. Charles Bell) perform well over the entire region, but most people prefer the pointed buds of some of the other roses. In the hybrid tea class, especially desirable in the arid Southwest, are Peace, Eclipse, Buccaneer, Golden Masterpiece, Fred Howard, Comtesse Vandal, Picture, Rubaiyat, Charlotte Armstrong, Helen Traubel, Mojave, Mme Henri Guillot, Tallyho, Mrs. Sam McGredy, Etoile de Hollande, Texas Centennial, New Yorker, Bravo, Poinsettia, McGredy's Ivory, K. A. Viktoria, and Rex Anderson.

Queen Elizabeth is the best of grandifloras noted for their hybrid-tea-shaped flowers which are borne in clusters and held on long cutting-length stems. Roundelay and Carrousel are also in this class and can be recommended for the area, as can Buccaneer which is exceptionally vigorous, has good flower form and color, but which is sometimes lacking in the cluster-flowering habit.

There are many varieties in the floribunda class of roses from which to choose. These all bear clusters of small-sized flowers with short stems, and some of the best are Fashion, Else Poulsen, Donald Prior, Eutin, Circus, Valentine, and Summer Snow.

IN THE NORTHWEST

Roses may be cut by gardeners seven months of the year in the general area referred to as the moist Pacific Northwest. Two weeks without rain brings out newspaper notices concerning the "drought" conditions. Winters are frequently so mild that planting operations continue through from November until March without interruption.

While it is conceded that roses enjoy plenty of water, certain varieties do not perform at their best under the almost excessive humidity of the Pacific Northwest. These varieties include roses of unusually numerous petals (generally over fifty). This is especially true when the petal texture is thin. In such cases, the blooms will not open well and will hang on the plant in an unsightly manner.

Roses having petals that overlap one another are also prone to follow this pattern. In addition to selecting roses of moderate petalage and heavy texture, rosarians of the Pacific Northwest have one more limitation placed upon them. Along with plenty of moist, cool days the area has a temperature range in summer which rarely exceeds 80 degrees. Nights are almost always cool (50-60 degrees). Roses that need warm days and nights to produce rich color have a tendency to show muddy, uninteresting blooms in the moderate climate. Such varieties as Mirandy (which is an unsightly purple) and Chief Seattle (a dull buff) rarely attract much favorable comment, except in an unusually warm summer. Most of the roses referred to in the catalogs as apricot or peach blend fall in the class above. It is certainly no disparagement of the varieties, only a climatic factor which must be carefully considered.

ROSES IN HIGH ALTITUDES

Most hybrid teas and floribundas will do well at the higher altitudes (4,000 to 7,000 feet) so long as proper winter protection is taken (see page 133). But, where should you buy a rose bush when you live at a high altitude? If there is a nurseryman in your community ask him where his stock comes from. If it has come from California, you can feel safe in buying. It is felt that roses grown in California on understock, such as Dr. Huey (Shafter Robin), Ragged Robin and *Rosa multiflora,* are best suited to high altitude conditions. If you do not purchase locally but through a mail-order catalog, be sure to find out what understock has been used.

The special care required by roses in the various sections of our country are fully covered in Chapters 4 through 8.

3

HOW TO USE ROSES
IN YOUR GARDEN

The modern rose, compact of habit and glossy of leaf, is a handsome plant, even out of bloom. It can be used, as shown, to brighten gardens in many ways.

Roses need not be assigned to an out-of-the-way bed, but can be included in a border for seasonal interest among other flowers. The traditional rose garden, with plants formally arranged in symmetrical planting beds, is not the best way to display the beauty of this flower in the home garden. Although their care is somewhat easier when they are grouped together, the plant with its flowers has an engaging informal quality that can thus be lost. See how attractive roses are, grown here on fences and walls or as specimens among other plants.

If you do decide to plant them in beds, an informal design is best for most gardens. The outline of the bed should be a definite and well proportioned shape that will be attractive during the winter, when the area is covered with a mulch. Even if the roses are in a cutting garden away from public view, it is more of a pleasure to work with them in an attractive setting.

REQUIREMENTS FOR ROSE PLANTING

Before you actually start to lay out the plans for your rose garden, it is a good idea to know your wants against the rose's needs.

LOCATING THE PLANTING

You can start with the best quality stock of rose varieties of the highest ratings, but they will perform in beauty only if they are given a compatible location. Roses are plants of the sun. In fact, roses attain their best growth in full sunshine, but good results may be obtained if they are exposed to sunshine for at least 6 to 8 hours a day. (In some of the more southern states where sunlight is very intense, fine roses can be grown where they have only 4 hours of sun.) Where there is shade, it is far better to have it on the plants in the late afternoon. If the plants are in morning-shade, the foliage will remain wet with dew for a few hours longer than if in direct sunlight, and the presence of moisture on the leaves is a very favorable condition for the development of several leaf-diseases. Also, be sure not to place the rose garden close to trees with matted surface roots, such as maples, elms, and poplars. This disadvantage can be partly corrected by cutting the tree roots along the edge of the rose bed several times a year. Although roses should not be planted in a dead-air pocket (stagnant air encourages disease), they need some protection from high winds. Hedges, shrub borders, walls, or fences can provide this windbreak.

SOIL REQUIREMENTS

Any good garden soil will produce good roses. If good grass, shrubs, and other plants will grow in the garden, it is practically certain that no special treatment of the soil is necessary for roses. There is, however, some preference for silty

Figure 16   Roses on a fence are a garden in themselves. Here they are used picturesquely near a stone cottage, and as you pass them you know that the people of the house cherish tradition. Because the roses are used with restraint and do not hide the fence, you know the owners have an artistic sense, and because the roses are cared for and healthy, it is obvious that gardeners live here.

55

Figure 17 A rose garden enclosed in a boxwood hedge. It is in a good sunny location, an important consideration when planning a r
garden.

clay or clay loam; the lighter sands should be avoided. The optimum pH value of
the soil for roses is between 5.0 and 7.0, which is slightly on the acid side.
Very acid or very alkaline soils are unsuitable. Methods of correcting problem
soils are fully covered in the next chapter.

Good soil drainage is most important in the successful growing of roses.
Poorly drained soils, or any location where water accumulates after every rain,
will not produce good roses. Also, do not plant roses on a *steep* hillside where
runoff makes watering difficult.

56

To check the drainage of a prospective rose site, dig a hole about a foot deep. Then fill the hole with water. If all the water drains away in an hour or so, the drainage is acceptable. If, on the other hand, most of the water still remains in the hole, some type of drainage arrangement is required. Should water seep into the dug hole of its own accord, the local water table at that location is too high for good results with roses.

Three methods may be employed to correct a poor drainage situation.

1. If the water ran out of your test hole rather slowly, the drainage generally can be improved by putting down a 6- to 8-inch layer of crushed stone or gravel under the rose garden at a depth of 12 to 24 inches.

2. Should little or no water seep out of the test hole, the installation of 3-inch drain tile should be made to about 20 inches below the soil surface. If a large area is involved, the tile should be spaced 6 to 10 feet apart, depending on how poor the drainage is. The tile should be sloped about 3 inches for every 10 feet, and some provision should be made to drain off the water carried by the tile to a sump filled with stones. A bed of crushed stone should be located under the plants, as previously mentioned, and tile arranged so that it collects the water from the gravel layer.

3. Where the water table is high, it is possible to elevate the planting level or grade so that the roses' roots are above the water level.

SPACING OF THE PLANTS

The spacing of rose plants depends on several factors, including the variety of the rose, the climate in which it is grown, the method of pruning to be used, and the type of bush desired. There is considerable difference in vigor among the varieties. A strong grower, such as Crimson Glory, may require twice as much space as many others. It is now believed by most experts that hybrid tea roses should be spaced at least 2 feet or more in sections where winterkilling of the canes is not severe and it is possible to grow rather large bushes. Where the climate is so severe that the plants are usually winterkilled back to a few inches above the soil, it is advisable to plant somewhat closer. In any case, enough space should be allowed so the plants can develop fully and receive as much sunlight and aeration as possible. Such spacing provides room for good culture and for spraying or dusting operations to control diseases and insects. Plants that have ample room also produce more and better flowers, and it is more economical to plant a bed properly with twenty-five plants than to crowd in thirty-five or forty. Generally, hybrid teas, polyanthas, grandifloras, and floribundas should be planted about 2 feet apart in areas where the winters are very cold, about 2½ feet apart in sections with mild winters, and at least 3 feet apart in the Southern and Pacific Coast states. Hybrid perpetuals should be spaced from 3 to 5 feet apart and climbers from 6 to 8 feet apart.

It is always well to recognize one's personal limitations and not to try to grow more plants than time and strength will permit one to tend. Twenty-five well grown roses will give far more pleasure than fifty that are inadequately tended. Five hundred plants is about the maximum a family can manage without extra help and with the average amount of free time they have in the evenings and weekends.

PLANNING THE ROSE GARDEN

Planning a rose garden can be a great deal of fun. The illustrations in this book show simple, informal groupings of roses, as well as complete, large formal rose gardens. You can use parts of these ideas, as well as variations. You can make your own plans—it is surprisingly easy. You can plan an expandable garden, and add some roses each year. You can learn about the other flowers that go well with roses. Looking through the pictures is a good way to start.

As you take your walking tour through the pictures, here are some pointers:

1. Do not restrict your thinking and your ideas to things you might do right away in your garden. Think how they might be applied to your neighbor's garden (this is part of the learning process). Learn to see the garden-design ideas that even large public gardens have. Eventually they will affect your own garden, even if only in small ways.
2. Be aware, as you translate picture ideas to actual land situations, of *sunlight*. Where is the shade? Where is the all-day sun?

58

Figure 18   Different kinds of roses as well as different colors can be beautifully combined in the garden. Hybrid teas, floribundas, and tree roses are happily related in this garden.

3. Think in terms of level areas, or ways you can feasibly level a sloping area. Beware of too many rocks and stones. Think of drainage—roses need the kind of soil and the kind of location that do not create long-standing puddles. (At times, you can plant on a hillside—if you plan for it.) Also, think in the terms of expanding your plantings. Once you have started a rose garden, chances are you will want to have new rose varieties at various times. Sometimes it is wise to plan your garden in step-by-step fashion over a several-year period.

4. Think of one other practical aspect of a rose bed: accessibility for planting, cultivating, pruning, and spraying. A bed more than 5 feet across is usually too difficult to get at for necessary work. If a wider effect is desired, make two narrow beds side by side with a service walk of stepping stones between them.

5. Think of the purpose of a rose bed, a row of roses, or a whole garden of roses. If it is purely decorative from a moderate distance, keeping masses of one color is desirable. This affects not only the choice of the roses you buy, but also the ideas you get in planning a bed. If, on the other hand, you want a combination of a display of roses, a place to cut flowers for indoor use, and the extra pleasure of growing several new kinds of roses, choose the right kind of location for such a multipurpose bed. A row of low floribundas along a driveway is fine—but the same space devoted to roses of different colors, different heights, and different blooming times would look bedraggled, no matter how beautiful the individual plants were.

6. Think in terms of *informal*—or *formal*. You can have both on the same property, but in general it takes skill, practice, and knowledge of just how each kind of plant grows to work out combinations of the two.

These principles, of course, are ways to approach the whole subject. They are pointers on how to look at a rose garden; as you learn to see the meanings of these pointers in gardens you visit, your mind will be learning how to design —and a very pleasant experience it is. There are other principles of garden design that in time you will learn—some will be a little arty with less emphasis on practical points—but these finer approaches work only for someone who knows the practical points thoroughly.

Other ideas that you will get can be simply larger-scale projections of our starting point—the simple corner. For example, think of a small rose garden, or a rose border that is part of a larger garden setting. It does not take much thinking to decide that a table and chairs of attractive garden furniture should

Figure 19 The floribunda, Fashion, combined with violas, makes an interesting and colorful garden.

be located near the fragrance and the color of the roses—so try to think of that area as outdoor living-room space.

One home gardener planned three borders, as edges around a square of grass. In one corner, under a tree, he placed a small square—perhaps 8 feet by 10—of flagstones, as the outdoor living-room space. One border was full of perennials, the other two were roses. The first rose border had a white-fence background; against this a row of pink Robin Hood roses were planted, with their small flowers in spilling-over clusters to complete the background. Hybrid teas were in front of the row of Robin Hood, and they were kept pruned low.

The other rose border was against the white, brick-wall side of a garage. Climbers were in the back, and both hybrid teas and floribundas in the front row.

The whole effect was pleasant—not completely formal, and not as good from a landscape standpoint as though groups of all white or all red roses had been used. But the constant bloom from early June to the end of September made the "sitting garden" a useful and pleasant place.

When planning your rose garden, consider the view of it from fortunately located windows. Bring it into your home through the windows. Also, consider companion plants for your rose garden, since if properly selected they can add

61

to the attractiveness of the plan. Plants like sweet alyssum can add fragrance to the garden when the roses are not fully in bloom. Also, do not forget that roses are deciduous and are not at their prettiest when leafless. Therefore, use low evergreen plants in the foreground or tall ones in the background to attract the eye when the rose plants are dormant.

COMPANION PLANTS FOR ROSES

Edging

Ageratum	Lobelia: 4 inches
King of Blues: 6 inches	Mignonette, dwarf: 6 inches
Midget Blue: 3 inches	Nierembergia: 8 to 10 inches
Alyssum, Sweet	Phlox, dwarf: 6 inches
Carpet of Snow: 4 inches	Torenia: 10 inches
Royal Carpet (purple): 4 inches	Verbena, dwarf: 10 inches
Browallia: 12 inches	*Viola cornuta*

Taller Plants

Baby's-breath (Gypsophila)	Lily
Clematis	Lupine
Delphinium	Petunia
Dianthus	Rosemary
Germander	Sideritis
Heliotrope	Stock
Lavender	Thermopsis

Elsewhere in this book are pointers on growing roses, on selecting varieties, and on their care. Even these facts fit into the problem of how to use them in a garden; but for the moment let us concentrate on the types of roses and how to use them.

Floribundas are more informal and give more of a mass effect than hybrid teas. In garden design, use them for what they are. Use them as an edge for a large rose border. For instance, use floribundas around the cottage-type of house, perhaps as a foundation planting. One variety is enough—usually a floriferous kind of strong color like Fashion, Geranium Red, or Orange Ruffles. Another congenial locale for these roses is around the border of a vegetable or flower garden. The taller-growing floribundas or grandifloras used as a hedge or trained along a wire fence outline the property strikingly.

As for climbing roses—if you have a trellis, a porch pillar that is suitable, a fence, why of course you think of climbers. Or, to turn the idea around, if you love climbing roses, you must find or create situations for them. You will get a bigger splash for your money from a few climbers than from any other kind of rose plant, and most times you will do less caretaking work.

The hybrid tea rose grower has another kind of problem. These are the queens of rosedom, because of perfection of form in the individual blossoms. But this very perfection is obtained at a price—less of a splash of color if you really work at making single blossoms show at their best. So how do you handle them in designing the garden?

Answer: Not so close up, as far as plants are concerned; not so prominent; not right out in front of the footlights and spotlight, so to speak. But when they are cut for display inside the house, then you get your closeup. This means, in garden design, that the garden of a hybrid tea specialist is less likely to look as good from a medium distance. You can plant the beds for walking around, to show your guests the choice flowers. You can keep them farther away from

Figure 20 A rose-perennial garden located on the seashore. Bushes need special winter care to protect them against the cold wind.

63

Figure 21 When planning any garden, be sure to consider how it looks from inside your window.

everyday traffic. You can put edges of splashy floribundas around them to make up for their less dramatic way of life "at the middle distance."

Do not forget about grandifloras in your plant. Because of their vigorous growth, they form excellent hedges or screens. They can also be used as background plants or as pillars for accent. Remember that, like the hybrid tea, the grandiflora bloom is highly valued as a cut flower for decorative purposes.

There are other ways of looking at roses in garden design that merit your thoughtful eye. As shrubs, for example, where you can use one plant or a group in a very informal way. You can use old-fashioned roses (see Chapter 1 on this

Figure 22 A garden seat is surrounded by an arbor, a bed of hybrid teas, and a trellis.

subject) and let the plants blend into the landscape when the flowers are not in bloom. You can use many kinds of roses for hedges, for screens, or a change of pace in a distant part of the garden.

Still another variation to keep in mind is the rose in a tub or pot. In such a container, it can be moved to the patio when you want it. It can be cared for on a terrace or a deck easily and placed just where it ought to be. It will give a special kind of ornamental touch to the architecture of the garden. It can even be used to fill in for a plant that has died. Some home gardeners plant roses in tubs for one season, and then plant them out in a permanent bed. The choice of containers is wide and includes ceramic, wood, or plastic. Redwood boxes can be built at home (see page 82).

All in all, your seeing eye learns to look for roses, and for places where roses go well, as you progress further down the gardening path. Recognition of the varieties of roses will be one pleasure; the feeling for the characteristic size and shape of types and even individual varieties will grow in your mind. You will learn about the glossy, big leaves of Peace roses, and the delicate, soft green tracery of some moss roses, or the red-to-green variations of Chrysler Imperials. You will get ideas for using this special foliage knowledge in "sculpturing with plants," as you make changes in your garden design.

Most of all, perhaps you will learn the eventual "secret" of garden design: The fun of it is in the fact it never ends. Nature keeps changing the plants; the people who use the garden keep changing; and your own ideas as well as your own design of the garden keep changing too. It is a growth—just like roses themselves enjoy. So get out your pad and pencil—from here on in, it is up to you. Of course, if you need help, remember that your local nurseryman or garden center usually has a qualified consultant available. If the garden is to be elaborate and economy not the overriding factor, hire a landscape architect to help in the planning of your rose garden.

BACKGROUND PLANTS FOR ROSE GARDEN BORDERS

Clipped Hedges (6' or taller)	Massing Shrubs (6' or taller)

DECIDUOUS

Aronia arbutifolia
Red Chokeberry

*Cinnamomum camphora
Camphor-tree

Cydonia japonica
Japanese Quince

Crataegus crus-galli
Cockspur Thorn

†Forsythia intermedia
Border Forsythia

Fagus sylvatica
European Beech

*†Hibiscus orsa-sinensis
Chinese Hibiscus

Forsythia intermedia
Border Forsythia

Ilex verticillata
Winterberry

Ligustrum ovalifolium
California Privet

Kolkwitzia amabilis
Beautybush

*Nerium oleander
Common Oleander

*Lagerstroemia indica
Crape-myrtle

*Poncirus trifoliata
Hardy-orange

Lonicera fragrantissima
Winter Honeysuckle

*Prunus laurocerasus
English Cherry-laurel

†Philadelphus coronarius
Sweet Mock-orange

Syringa vulgaris
Common Lilac

†Rhodotypos scandens
Jetbead

Ulmus pumila
Dwarf Asiatic Elm

Rosa multiflora
Japanese Rose
(prune back annually)

EVERGREEN

†Spiraea vanhouttei
Vanhoutte Spirea

*Euonymus japonica
Evergreen burningbush

†Syringa vulgaris
Common Lilac

Ilex crenata
Japanese Holly

†Viburnum dilatatum
Linden Viburnum

Ilex opaca
American Holly

Viburnum tomentosum
Doublefile Viburnum

* Especially for warm climates.
† May be used as informal hedge.

EVERGREEN (*cont.*)

Ligustrum lucidum
　　Glossy Privet
Picea orientalis
　　Oriental Spruce
Pinus strobus
　　Eastern White Pine
Pittosporum tobira
　　Japanese Pittosporum
Taxus baccata
　　English Yew
Thuja occidentalis
　　American Arborvitae
Tsuga canadensis
　　Canada Hemlock

COLOR IN THE ROSE GARDEN

One of the loveliest pleasures a rose garden offers is its appeal to our sense of color. Yet many gardens are less effective than they would be if color were more carefully considered.

Certainly, color nomenclature is in a state of confusion so far as roses are concerned. Various catalog descriptions of the same rose may be entirely different, as catalog writers may not agree upon the exact color of a certain variety. Also, location and soil help to determine the specific shade of many roses. So you cannot always be sure just what color rose you will get.

Many rose growers speak only of definite color groups; to them a rose is red, pink, yellow, white, or bicolor. But what about the intermediate shades? Red Radiance, Charlotte Armstrong, Mirandy, Nocturne, Crimson Glory, and

* Especially for warm climates.

68

Figure 23　An interesting floribunda-hedge arrangement around a garden wall.

Chrysler Imperial are all "red" roses, although they may vary from a light red to a blackish crimson or maroon. The pinks and yellows vary as greatly as the reds in shades and intensity of color. Even in the whites, which have the least variations, we find various tints of pink, yellow, and green.

HARMONY OR CONTRAST

What makes a good color combination? Even the least sensitive person finds certain combinations objectionable and others pleasing. You have combined colors well if you produce harmony or contrast. Harmony is obtained by balancing colors of similar shades; contrast, by using entirely different colors. Harmony is more restful to the eye than contrast, but under some conditions contrasting colors are desirable.

When a considerable number of roses are to be planted, with wide paths left between the beds, the simplest way to enjoy their color is to plant one variety in each bed. However, if roses of several different colors are planted in one large bed, the colors will not clash as readily as would a few colors in a small bed. The association of a variety of colors in a mass does not allow the eye to form an impression of either harmony or contrast. Yet, when only two unassociated colors are planted together, the eye is able to compare one with the other and register the impression that the combination is not a pleasing one.

There are a number of miniature and dwarf polyantha roses now available for border accents and many attractive shrub roses for background plantings, but there are some instances where other plants may be used to advantage. If a desired color combination is not obtainable with roses alone, certain other flowers that will blend in color can be associated with them. These, however, should be relegated to the role of embellishments and used only in borders or in the background. Violas, pansies, portulaca, English daisies, nigellas, nemesias, and other low-growing material may be used for bordering rose beds. Save tall-growing plants for the background; clumps of sweet peas planted alternately with pillar roses give a pleasing effect. Try to select plants whose best display of bloom coincides with that of the roses or plants that have a long flowering period.

70

BLENDING COLORS

The successful blending of colors in the rose garden is not a difficult problem, as the color range of the genus *Rosa* reaches from the snow white of Frau Karl Druschki to the deep blackish crimson of Night. There are even shades of blue, violet, purple, lavender, and gray in some varieties such as Violette, Cardinal de Richelieu, Gray Pearl, Sterling Silver, and Twilight.

For best effects, keep dark varieties away from dark backgrounds, because when they are so placed, their coloring is lost. It is better to group them among white, yellow, or light pink varieties. Scarlet-crimsons do not show to best advantage when planted near crimson-maroons or deep velvety crimsons. If the predominating color is red, paler varieties should also be planted to provide contrast.

When pink is the paramount color, the bed may be highlighted by planting, here and there, a variety having blooms of scarlet or flame. The orange and yellow shades also help to pep up the pinks. The carmine pinks, in particular, should have white or pale yellow for contrast. Roses with marked hues of orange, terra cotta, and similar shades should be planted near cream or white varieties. White, cream-colored, and soft yellow roses will harmonize with almost any other color.

For a pleasing effect, plant salmon-pinks near varieties with blooms of rich orange, cerise, or flame. Here they show to better advantage than if planted with the light pinks, whites, or yellows. The pale pinks may gradually deepen to the full rose pinks and should be kept apart from the flesh and salmon-pink types. The pale pinks, however, look good in association with the dark crimson roses. In mixing pinks, the effect is better if the softer and richer shades are blended with brighter colors.

As a rule, the brightly colored varieties are most popular for massing, but you can achieve a delicate and restful effect by grouping the softer or paler shades. Although we prefer a bright color in an individual rose, we believe that a bed of softer colors is far more pleasing to the eye.

BICOLORS, FLORIBUNDAS AND POLYANTHAS

You can obtain a most vivid display by grouping together various bicolors that have a preponderance of rich shades. The bicolors are attractive in themselves, and it is difficult to find a place for them in beds of one-tone roses. The alternative seems to be to plant them in a bed by themselves so that each bush may be admired as a unit rather than the bed as a whole.

Polyantha and floribunda roses, particularly, offer endless possibilities as bedding subjects, if thought is given to the color scheme at planting time. Their color range is great and they offer attractive, more or less permanent plant material for homeowners, parks, and cemeteries. Vary good types are Else Poulsen, Karen Poulsen, Golden Salmon, Gloria Mundi, Belvedere, Goldilocks, The Fairy, Mrs. Joseph Hiess, and Orange Triumph. It is not advisable to mix polyanthas and floribundas with hybrid teas; they are much more effective when planted in separate beds. In fact, it is never advisable to plant roses of more than one type in a single bed, as the habit of growth differs too greatly.

Figure 24   Tubs of roses at the edge of a terrace will give you a rose garden if space does not permit you to grow them elsewhere. The tubs lend sculptural interest and their color does not clash with the roses. Evergreen branches among the plants in winter look good and form a good protection.

72

4

HOW TO PLANT ROSES

Roses are not difficult to establish and there is no great mystery about their needs. There is, of course, a *right* way to plant a rose bush—and it is the purpose of this chapter to give you the few simple techniques that should be followed to insure a successful planting. But, remember, it is rather hard to go wrong in setting out rose plants.

TIME TO PLANT

Roses growing in pots or containers may be planted any time when the soil can be worked. This is one of the major reasons for the increasing popularity of potted roses. Bare-root roses, on the other hand, are planted either at the end of the season, just after becoming dormant, or at the beginning of the next season, before the bud break. Actually, there is considerable disagreement among rosarians as to whether spring planting or fall planting is the most satisfactory. In fact, it is impossible to state arbitrarily that any particular time of planting is best. First, what is best for one section may be undesirable for another. Secondly, what may happen in one season, from a weather standpoint, may not occur the next. The beginner who is in doubt as to the best time to plant in his section should obtain the advice of local rose growers.

In general, fall planting, or later, is believed best in areas where the winters are relatively mild. In very cold sections, the temperature usually drops too early in the fall for newly planted roses to become established before severe freezing. Under such conditions, spring planting is necessary. In sections where the winters are mild, roses may be planted at any time when they are fully dormant, your decision usually depending upon personal preference and convenience. In the South, where the dormant period is short, planting may be done from November (best for Florida) to February. In California, which also has a short dormant period, the planting period is early January to late February.

When a rose garden is to be established or when only a few plants are added to the planting, the soil should be prepared in advance and the spot where each plant is to be placed located with a stake. If the soil needs to be completely reworked, this should be done in the fall—for either spring or fall plantings. For fall plantings, the soil should be reworked four to six weeks before the plants are set out.

As we stated in Chapter 3, any good garden soil will produce good roses. If good grass, shrubs, and other plants will grow in the garden, it is practically certain that no special treatment of the soil is necessary for roses. When, however, the soil is known to be very poor, as is the case when the subsoil from a basement excavation has been used to level off a building lot, special soil preparation is necessary. Either heavy soil or sandy soil lacking fertility can be greatly improved by the addition of organic matter. Organic matter includes any decaying plant or animal refuse, such as peat, leafmold, or well-rotted manure. In some instances it may be advisable to remove a layer of soil 12 to 18 inches deep and mix it thoroughly with well-rotted manure in the proportion of about six bushels of soil to one of manure. Peat or leafmold, if used, should be mixed in the proportion of one part peat or leafmold to four parts of soil. It is also usually advisable to mix thoroughly with the 7-bushel mixture of soil and manure about one-half pound of superphosphate or bone meal.

Soils that do not require such extensive treatment can be greatly improved by spreading organic matter evenly over the soil surface and working it in to about the depth of a spade length. The amount to apply will vary with the condition of the soil, but 2 to 4 inches of peat, leafmold, or well-rotted manure will be beneficial.

PLANTING BARE-ROOT PLANTS

Ninety percent of the roses planted in the United States are still planted with bare-root stock. While potted roses are increasing in popularity, most roses are planted in the bare-root, dormant stage.

Bare-root plants should be set out as soon as they are received. If this is not possible, the plants should be unpacked and examined to see if the roots have dried out. If the sphagnum or other packing material about the roots is dry, it should be moistened and replaced, provided planting is not delayed more than a few days. If it is necessary to delay planting longer than a few days, the plants should be unpacked and heeled in, that is, placed in a trench and the roots covered with moist soil. If the roots are dry when received, they should be soaked in water for several hours before heeling them in. If the stems are also dry, the condition of the plants may sometimes be improved by burying them for a few days in moist soil. If plants are received in a frozen condition, they should be stored where they will thaw out gradually and should not be unpacked until completely free from frost.

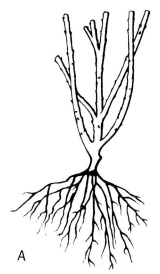

When all preparations for planting have been made, the roots of each plant should be carefully examined. All dead or injured growth should be cut off. The top should also be pruned, if needed. Generally nurseries cut back the tops of roses to about 12 inches before shipping them. Any dead or injured wood should be removed. If stems are cut back to less than 10 inches, flowering is usually delayed. Also, do not trim the canes of tree roses, climbers, or ramblers.

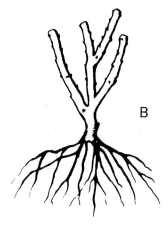

When the plants are ready to be set out, take them to the garden with their roots covered. The roots should never be exposed to the sun or drying winds. Failure to protect the roots at this time may result in very poor growth of the plants or even death. Plants should be moved to the planting ground in a bucket, their roots covered with water or puddled in a thin mixture of clay mud, and then kept covered with wet burlap or some other protection until planted.

Prepare all the planting holes at the same time and to the same depth. This insures regular spacing and uniform planting. The holes should be made about 12 inches deep and at least 18 inches in diameter. Completely loosen the soil at the bottom of each hole, and, if the soil is very poor, about a half spadeful of well rotted manure may be worked in at this time. Fresh manure

Figure 25 A rose bush (A) as it comes from the nursery. The same rose bush (B) ready to plant with top thinned and roots shortened slightly.

75

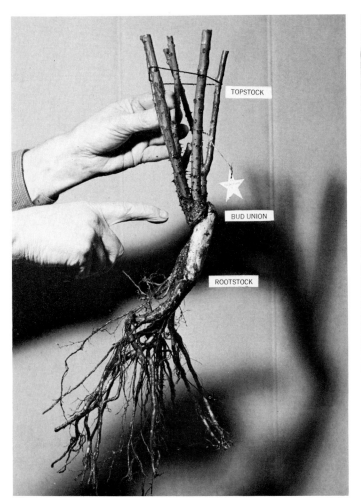

Figure 26   The bud union *(left)* is the major consideration when planting a rose. The rose bush (right) in the center planted correctly. The bush at the bottom is too deep while the one at the top is too shallow.

must be used with caution, since it may injure any roots coming in contact with it. A small cone-shaped pile of soil at the center of the planting hole is helpful in placing the roots and setting the plant at the proper depth.

There is nothing mysterious about the proper depth to plant a rose bush, if the reason for the recommendations are understood. The rose you buy is made up of two parts: the *understock,* a plant chosen for the hardiness and vigor of its roots; and *topstock,* developed and selected for its beauty and performance. In the nursery the young understock is planted out in the fields in spring. Then in summer the bark of the stem is slit and a small bud of the selected topstock is inserted. This junction is known as the bud union. The understock continues to grow during the summer. The following spring the growth from the understock that grew above the bud union is removed, leaving the chosen topstock variety to begin its development on the hardy root or understock. The vital point of any rose is the "bud union" or "knuckle" at the base of the canes. If this union is injured by cold, the topstock may die. In cold climates the union must be protected by planting 2 inches below the surface of the soil. In mild climates protection from cold is not necessary, and exposure of the bud union to the sun produces more basal "breaks" (canes) from the base of the plant. Many gardeners in regions where temperatures seldom go below zero are finding it best to plant with the bud union at soil level or slightly above. This is contrary to directions given some years ago.

Place the bush on the cone of soil in the hole so that the crown rests on the top and the roots spread naturally down its slope. Cover the roots with soil and push it firmly down with either a blunt stick or your fingers. It is important that no air pockets be left around the roots.

When the hole is two-thirds filled with soil, tramp it down with your foot and then fill the remainder of the hole with water. After the water has soaked in, the hole can be filled level with surrounding soil and again watered for further settling. The key word in planting a rose bush is firmness. Remember that loosely planted roses will soon die.

To prevent the canes from drying out before the roots are established, mound the soil up around them to a height of 8 to 10 inches. Firm the mound with the hands and wet it down with a fine spray. After the first new growth appears or when all danger of freezing is past, the soil above ground level should be removed. But when removing the mound, do so with caution, so as not to injure the new shoots. Also, remember that a newly planted rose must be well watered to keep the soil around the roots moistened.

After planting a tree rose, attach the central stem to a supporting stake with a slightly loose loop of strong cord, or use one of those special loop devices made for this purpose, which are available at most nurseries and garden centers. Ramblers and climbers should be securely but loosely fastened to the fence or arbor that they will be growing upon.

In the South, two variations from usual planting methods are followed. First, provide a 3-inch deep "dish" around each plant to contain the mulch and for ease of watering. Second, plant the bush "as it grew in the field." This means the graft bud may be several inches out of the soil. The bud is perfectly hardy without cover in the South, and when it is exposed, the plant will grow sturdier and new canes will break more readily. Nothing is more discouraging to a Southern rose than a smothered bud.

A

B

C

D

E

F

G

Figure 27   Steps in planting a rose: (A) Dig a hole at least a foot deep and a foot or more wide for each plant. (B) Spread out the roots, raying them downward over a cone of earth. (C) Work the soil about the roots. Keep graft union just below surface except in very mild climates, where it should be level with soil surface. (D) Firm the soil carefully about plant with hands; then firm more by treading with foot—the firmer the better. Loosely planted roses will soon die. (E) Slowly run water into hole and allow it to completely soak in. Add more water until no more will be readily absorbed. Then fill the hole with soil. (F) At the normal ground level, or an inch or two below, fertilize with a standard fertilizer or with bone meal or manure. Special rose fertilizers also can be used to advantage. (G) Finally, hill-up the soil about base of plants to keep canes from drying while roots become established. When growth starts, remove all of this soil.

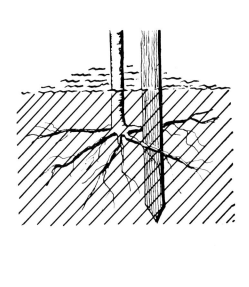

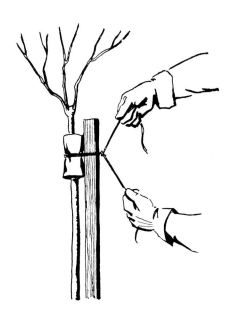

Figure 28 (*top-left*) When setting out a standard or tree rose, firmly drive a stake close to the main stem. (*bottom-left*) The stake should reach to top of the stem. The bark may be protected with cloth or plastic. (*right*) A properly staked rose tree.

Fill the "dish" with a good mulch, such as strawy cow manure, ground corncobs, or aged sawdust, but if peat moss is used, cover it with pine straw to prevent caking and drying out.

Beginning in early April and continuing through September, water thoroughly. This means placing the hose in the "dish" and letting the water run slowly until the mulch floats and the water comes up to the surface of the ground. Do this once a week unless there has been well over an inch of rain. If in doubt, use the hose.

More and more roses are being sold in cans, pots, or tarpaper containers. They may be planted any time the soil is workable. To plant, follow these seven simple steps:

PLANTING A POTTED ROSE

1. Dig a hole six inches larger all around the rose container. Place a half cupful of fertilizer (see page 87) in the bottom of the hole.

2. Mix the fertilizer with the soil in the hole bottom. Remember that the roots should not come into direct contact with the fertilizer.

3. Cut down the container on opposite sides if the nurseryman did not do it for you. Then carefully remove the plant from the slit container so as not to injure the roots.

4. In the South, set the plant with the top of the soil ball level with the ground; in the North, set it about two inches deeper.

5. Replace the soil around the root ball, and firm carefully with your foot to eliminate all pockets of air.

6. Fill the hole with water or with a so-called starter solution—two tablespoons of regular fertilizer to a gallon of water, or one of the soluble forms mixed according to directions. After the water or solution has soaked in, level the soil about the bush.

7. Apply a light mulch (see page 74) after watering to conserve moisture. Water at least once a week during the summer.

PLANTING A ROSE IN A CONTAINER

As we illustrated on several occasions in this book, roses can be planted in containers for patio and terrace use. True, roses cannot be considered as great container plants, but given proper care (see page 91) they can be grown quite successfully in tubs, pots, and boxes.

Figure 29 Roses, when properly planted and cared for, will grow nicely in redwood containers.

Floribundas—like Red Pinocchio, Goldilocks, Betty Priar, Circus, Zambra, Spartan, Sunport, Fire King, Fashion, Rumba, Saratoga, Redgold, Europeana, Angel Face, and Gene Boerner—make the best rose-container plants. The container, whether wood, clay, or ceramic, must be large enough to hold sufficient amounts of soil and permit the plant to have an ample root system. Also container-grown roses need good soil. One soil mixture that seems to work well is as follows:

7 parts loam
1 part peat moss
1½ parts well-rotted cow manure

To this add a generous portion of bone meal.

Before planting the bush, carefully *prune* the root system back to about 8 to 10 inches. Fill the container about one quarter full with the soil mixture and then place the plant in the center. Spread out the roots in the soil, and add new soil. Be sure the plant is firmly set, as previously described, in the container. When the plant is finally set, the bud union should be about an inch above the soil surface, while the soil level should be about 2 inches below the rim of the container.

TRANSPLANTING ESTABLISHED ROSES

Transplanting of old and fairly large roses is not difficult. Under some circumstances, it actually seems to give a new lease on life to a plant that may have been languishing.

Transplanting should be done in fall or spring when the plant is as nearly dormant as possible. It is probably a matter of custom or of local conditions whether transplanting is done on a ball of earth or on bare root. In rainy fall weather in mild climates very little attention to retaining a ball on the root of the bush seems necessary. If the soil is dry and crumbly, perhaps balling is desirable. The ground around the bush should be soaked thoroughly in advance of digging, so that the ball will stick on the roots: the hole that is to receive the

83

transplant should be in readiness before the rose is dug. Whichever way is used, water the newly transplanted rose thoroughly into position and tramp the earth around it.

Before transplanting, prune the bush back sufficiently to balance the root system. How sharply it needs to be cut back depends upon whether it is a large grower or a weak grower, and how much of the root system is eliminated in the digging.

In areas of severe winter cold, climbing roses transplanted in fall should be fall pruned and the canes allowed to lie on the ground under protection until spring.

Actually any rose can be planted or transplanted at almost any time if thorough, careful, and continued watering is given. When transplanted during the growing season, the tops should be cut back to approximately one third their normal height, and, if possible, the plant should be sprayed with an anti-transpirant immediately after being cut back. Care should be taken to take as much earth with the roots as possible. It should be watered at once and regularly until it takes hold in its new location. It is also good practice to shade the plant from the sun for several days. Roses transplanted during the growing season will suffer considerable setback and will be lost to production of bloom for a good portion of that year.

5

CULTURE OF ROSES

In considering the culture of roses, remember one very important fact: It is the God-given purpose and intention of a rose bush to grow and produce bloom and fulfill its life cycle according to its nature, and ordinarily it will do this if you give it a chance. Sometimes it is as possible to send a rose into a decline by coddling it as it is by neglecting it. In other words, it is your job to help your roses, rather than to "baby" them. Once the bushes are planted in suitable location and soil, the job of maintenance can be so routine that the lady of the house can do it in her spare time, if the man of the house prefers some other hobby or exercise.

CULTIVATING AND MULCHING

The roots of roses are generally shallow and spreading. Therefore, cultivation should be only an inch or two deep and should be done with care. The main purpose of cultivation is to remove weeds which compete with the roses for nutrients as well as moisture. Weeding can be done by hand pulling or by cutting

Figure 30 Mulching improves a rose garden's appearance considerably but more than that it is an excellent way to avoid weeds and is effective in preventing blackspot. Mulches keep the soil temperatures even, during variations in the air temperature.

at the soil surface with a scuffle hoe. As growth begins in the spring a shallow working with a shovel will lay the foundation for easy surface cultivation through the remainder of the season.

If surface cultivation is relied upon for dust mulch to retain moisture and limit evaporation, the bed should be scratched with a rake or scuffle hoe after each heavy rain to prevent formation of a crust and keep the mulch character and function.

Most home gardeners now, however, use organic materials rather than surface cultivation on their beds as an aid in controlling weeds, conserving moisture, and adding fertility. Mulches of many materials have been used successfully on roses, including peat moss, wood chips and shavings, ground sugar cane, pine needles, compost, ground corncobs, ground tobacco stems, buckwheat and cottonseed hulls, spent mushroom manure, and well-rotted strawy manure, as well as combinations of these materials. The mulches are usually applied about a month before the roses bloom. They are spread evenly around the plants to a depth of 2 to 3 inches in Northern areas and to as much as 6 inches in the sandy soils of Florida and other parts of the Deep South. The reason for the wide variation is that sandy soils exposed to long periods of summer sunshine dry out more quickly and require additional mulch.

The mulch can go on early in the spring, after the spring pruning is done or from four to eight weeks before blooming time, and stay on through the season. In the fall or early the next spring, the mulch can be dug into the ground or removed and replaced. Many home gardeners retain a mulch throughout the year, adding new material as the mulch settles and becomes thin about the plants.

FERTILIZING

Roses are more often overfed than underfed. The average gardener, wishing to obtain the finest flowers, often believes he can accomplish his objective by heavy applications of fertilizers. A judicious use of fertilizers will aid in producing superior blooms, but fertilizers will not replace good general care, including proper watering and spraying for insect and disease control.

Roses will grow fairly well in many kinds of soil. However, they prefer a *slightly* acid soil. Therefore, a fine point in growing more perfect roses—especially hybrid teas—is the acidity of the soil.

How do you find out? What do you do about it? Both answers are fairly easy. With a soil test kit you can find the pH of your soil pretty quickly. Or your county agricultural agent or state university will make the test for you, at no charge.

The pH of the soil is the measure of alkalinity-acidity. A soil that is neutral (half-way between) has a pH of 7. If the value is lower than 7, the soil is acid; higher, it is alkaline. Roses grow best when the soil is slightly acid: 5.5 to 6.5. If the pH of the soil is lower, it may be raised by adding agricultural lime at the rate of about 3 to 4 pounds per 100 square feet. If the pH is over 6.5, the soil may be made acid by applying powdered sulfur at the rate of 1 to 3 pounds per 100 square feet, depending on how high the pH of the soil is. As a rule, 1 pound of sulfur per square feet is enough when the pH is 7 to 7.5. If the pH is 8, about 2 pounds of sulfur will be required, and for a reading of pH 8.5, about 3 pounds of sulfur should be applied. Since the pH value of soil can change rather quickly, it is advisable to recheck at monthly intervals after treating to see if another application of lime or sulfur is needed. If such procedures do not change the pH factor sufficiently, check with your county agricultural agent or state experiment stations for recommendations.

Good roses can be grown with little additional fertilization in a good fertile garden soil with a satisfactory pH value. If the soil is poor, the plants will soon show symptoms indicating a deficiency of one or more of the required fertilizer elements. Generally, most soils have ample quantities of all the necessary fertilizer elements except nitrogen, phosphorus, potassium, and sometimes calcium and iron. When the soil is deficient in nitrogen, the leaves, especially the younger ones, become yellow and are smaller than those on plants receiving ample quantities of nitrogen. When phosphorus is lacking, the leaves become grayish green, and a purplish tinge often appears on the underside. A deficiency of potassium is more difficult to diagnose because it may be confused with spray injury. Plants lacking potassium soon show a browning on the margins of the leaves, and sometimes a brown area appears on the flower stem just below the base of the flower.

Calcium deficiency causes the margin of the leaflets to die. Eventually the entire leaf dries and drops off. The flowers may be deformed with brown spots near the margins of the petals. When these symptoms appear, a soil test should be run. If the pH value is below 5, lime should be added to build up the calcium supply.

Iron is necessary for the formation of the green color in leaves. When iron is lacking, the leaves may become yellowish and the veins may stand out rather prominently.

Probably the best source of the elements needed by roses for growth, except calcium and iron, is the so-called complete or mixed inorganic fertilizers. They are sold in a wide range of mixtures, such as 5-10-5, 4-8-4, 4-8-6, 16-16-8, 12-24-12, or 10-20-10. The figures in each case indicate the percentage of nitrogen, phosphorus, and potassium, respectively, in the fertilizer. Thus a 5-10-5 fertilizer is one that contains 5 pounds of nitrogen, 10 pounds of phosphorus, and 5 pounds of potassium in every 100 pounds of mixture. As a rule, most soils are well supplied with iron. In some sections of the country, however, as on the

Great Plains, iron may be deficient, causing the rose foliage to turn yellowish white. This condition is known as iron chlorosis and is corrected by spraying the foliage with ferrous sulfate. This is used at the rate of 1 ounce of ferrous sulfate to 2 gallons of water.

When a complete inorganic fertilizer is used, it is advisable to apply it several times during the growing season. The first application should be made when the new spring growth is well established and all danger of severe freezing is past. If the plants show signs of deficiency later on, a second application may be made. Fertilizers should not be used in cold climates after July 15, and in mild climates after August 15. When used too late in the season they may stimulate fresh growth and delay hardening of the wood before winter sets in. In the Deep South, roses can be fed all year round, or about five to six feedings a year. Three is usually sufficient in the North.

In general, complete inorganic fertilizers are used at the rate of about 3 pounds per 100 square feet or a heaping tablespoonful for each plant. Spread the fertilizer evenly and scratch it into the soil or mulching material, preferably just before a rain or prior to watering the rose bed.

A rather recent development in complete inorganic fertilizer is the pellet form. A handful of these small, pea-sized pellets can be tossed exactly where you want them in your rose reds. In addition, being in pellet form, they dissolve slower than a powdered fertilizer and, as a result, their nutrient action is extended over a longer period of time with greater efficiency.

Organic fertilizers are good for roses, too. For instance, a top dressing of green barnyard manure in the fall—in rainy areas—is good, since the rains dilute and leach it into the soil without damage to the plants or loss of fertilizing value. Well-rotted stable manure is also recommended for a top dressing in the spring.

Liquid fertilizers are also good for summer rose feeding. There are numerous concentrated liquid fertilizers available, with adequate directions for dilution and application. Some of these are chemical formulae. Others are organic, such as fish emulsions. If you employ one of these liquids, be sure to follow the maker's directions as to application and schedule exactly, until you develop your own rule of thumb system.

"Leaf-feeding" or foliar fertilizers are being used by many rosarians with success. Here are four basic rules you should keep in mind when applying these leaf-feeding solutions:

1. Follow the maker's instructions on the label to the letter. Quantities used too strong or in excess of those amounts recommended could cause serious leaf damage.

2. Make certain to spray the undersides of the leaves thoroughly. Solution applied on the top sides is almost completely wasted.

3. When applying to a shiny-leafed variety, add a spreader-sticker (see page 97) to the solution to insure that the material will stay on these slick leaf surfaces.

4. The leaf-feeding program is generally started when the first leaves form in the spring, and the feeding schedule is carried on every two or three weeks through early July.

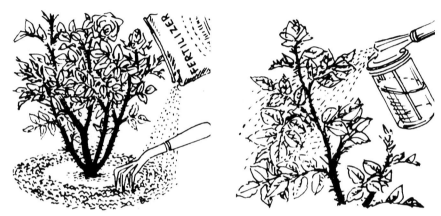

Figure 31   Applying fertilizer: Mix dry fertilizer with soil (*left*) or feed through leaves (*right*) with liquid applications. Start when growth begins in spring; repeat at monthly intervals until about two months before cold weather arrives. Always work dry fertilizer into soil, and water thoroughly.

WATERING

Watering is another requisite during any protracted period of dry weather. The feeding roots of a rose plant can take up only in soluble form the elements in the soil which the plant needs to manufacture its food. When watering is needed, soak the ground thoroughly to a depth of at least six inches. Sprinkling actually does more harm than good. If possible, avoid wetting the foliage. One simple method of watering is to allow the water to run directly onto the bed with the nozzle off the hose.

Among the modern devices that make irrigation easier is the water-wand, which attaches to the end of the hose and releases the water in an even flow directly at the base of the plant. A soil-soaker is another time-saving watering device. It consists of a porous canvas hose, which does a good deep watering job and can be moved easily from place to place. Overhead watering of plants should be done early enough in the day so that the foliage is dry by nightfall.

CONTAINER ROSE CULTURE

Roses grown in containers require more care than those raised in the open. As a rule, except in very hot weather, watering should be done every second or third day. Fertilizer should be applied about every two weeks after growth has started until July or August (see page 89). While liquid fertilizers are considered best for container plants, dry fertilizers that are *completely* water soluble can be used. Apply the dry fertilizer evenly, scratch it lightly into the soil, and water thoroughly.

Mulching is most important in container plant culture. It keeps surface roots cool and prevents excessive evaporation and drying out of the soil. Any of finer-grade mulch materials may be employed, and to improve the container's appearance, cover the mulch with a thin layer of coarse gravel or white marble chips.

Container roses usually require transplanting every second or third year. That is, they should be carefully dug out while dormant, root-pruned, and re-planted in newly prepared container soil (see page 83).

DISBUDDING

If large exhibition or single-stem roses are wanted, it is necessary to remove some of the flower buds. This is called disbudding. It should be done when the flower buds are very small. The terminal bud is usually selected and all other buds are removed. The terminal bud then develops into a much larger flower. You will learn by experience how to select buds weeks in advance for a special purpose. One time you may disbud the side shoots on a stem, at a very early stage, to get a long stem and a large flower. Another time you may cut a conflicting lateral off, so that it does not hurt the flower you especially want.

The flower clusters of floribundas and polyanthas, and any roses bearing many flowers per stem, will be improved by *partial* disbudding.

CUTTING THE FLOWERS

Cutting rose flowers is in itself an important cultural operation. Use sharp tools. Breaking or twisting off the flowers injures the remaining wood. The leaves of all plants are the factories in which the energy of the sun is used to manufacture food material used by the plant to produce more stems and leaves. Many home gardeners cut blooms with stems so long they rob the plant of too much of its manufacturing capacity, and thus cut down the growth and subsequent flower yield of their plants.

During the first season of bloom, the flowers should be cut with very short stems only. In fact some rosarians do not cut any flowers during the first season of bloom. If the early flowers are not cut, the plants will usually develop into large bushes by fall and some flowers may be cut then. Even when the plants are well established, it is unwise to cut stems any longer than actually needed. Leave at least two leaves between the cut and the main stem.

Hybrid tea roses usually have three leaflets at the top of the rose stem, and below that a spray of five leaflets. Make the cut just above the topmost spray of five leaflets if the stem is weak. If the stem is as thick as a pencil, the cut may be made above a higher three-leaflet spray.

If the flowers are not cut for home use, they should be removed when the petals fall. Cut them with sharp shears or a knife above the topmost leaf. A withered individual flower in a cluster should be removed to give the remaining flowers more room to develop. After all the flowers of a cluster have withered,

Figure 32 Cut roses with a pair of sharp shears; the cut is made just above a 5-leaflet leaf and at a 45-degree angle that slopes away from bud.

the entire stem should be cut off just above the top leaf. Remember: do not leave unkempt, ragged flowers on the plant. It is bad looking, and does not help the plant.

Roses that are cut just before the petals start to unfold will continue to develop normally and remain in good condition longer than if they are cut after they are fully open on the plant. Roses will also keep better when cut in the late afternoon or early evening. Early morning is next best. Indeed, the flower will be more fragrant if cut early in the day. At midday, however, there is less moisture in the stem and bud, and it will not last as long if it is cut at this time.

Here is a trick you should keep in mind when a problem similar to this presents itself: let us say that it is Thursday, and you have special company coming on Sunday. It has not rained for several days. Your hybrid teas have

93

many small, tight buds. The weather is warm and sunny, but your experience tells you the flowers will not even begin to open by Sunday. What to do? Get out the garden hose or the soil soaker. Set it at the base of the two or three plants that you want to flower. Let the water trickle slowly for hours and hours, thoroughly soaking the roots. Keep it up. By Saturday your roses will be growing furiously. On Saturday night, cut them and store with the stems in cold water in a cool, moist place. This will "harden" them.

This is the ideal way to have perfect blooms. Sometimes you have to go even further. You can hold back buds that are developing too quickly by keeping them at refrigerator temperature (but wrapped in tissue paper so the petals do not touch the refrigerator). This is what florists do. You can also speed up the opening by keeping them a few hours in tepid water.

Flowers that start to wilt prematurely indoors can be revived and their usefulness extended for several days. Make a slanting cut an inch or so up from the base of the stem, and place the stems in very hot water for a few minutes. Boiling water removed from the stove for a few minutes is satisfactory. Then plunge the stems quickly into cold water. The hot water drives off any air bubbles that may have formed in the water-conducting tissues of the stems and permits the cold water to rise and revive the flower. This treatment will not revive old flowers that have reached the full extent of their usefulness, or flowers that have been wilted for several hours. The use of chemical extenders such as *Floralife* or *Bloomlife* in the water will help prolong the flower's life. Also, keeping them in the refrigerator overnight will help to extend their lives.

6

KEEPING THE ROSES HEALTHY

The healthier your rose garden is, the less special attention it will require in the matter of disease and insect control. The health of roses depends primarily upon a good sunny location in proper, well-drained soil, adequate fertilization, sufficient water, and good air circulation. Since it is rather difficult—if not impossible —to have all these conditions to perfection, you must carry on a health program of spraying or dusting to control disease and insect pests.

THE TOOL FOR THE HEALTH PROGRAM

There are a few general measures that will be effective in solving most of the disease and insect problems of roses. These measures are rather simple. All that is needed are a good duster or sprayer, and a few insecticides and fungicides or a combination of both.

Whether you dust your roses or spray them in your health program is a matter of your own taste and convenience. Both methods are effective, each has many points in its favor and some against, and all such points sooner or later are resolved in relation to what the gardener himself finds most convenient and acceptable.

Among the dusters, there are several types you might consider. There is the plunger kind that is operated just like a small sprayer—push in the handle and a puff of dust comes out. There are also the rotary dusters, which give a continuous cloud of dust just as long as you keep turning the crank.

Gardeners with large collections of plants may turn to sprayers, since one filling will cover many plants. The small, plunger sprayer—the kind used for household spraying—is generally inadequate for spraying roses. It is best to consider one of the pressure sprayers. These sprayers, holding from 1 to 4 gallons of mixed spray, are operated by pumping up a pressure inside the tank so that the spray is released in a fine mist or stream. Many improvements have been made in these sprayers over the past few years.

There are other types of sprayers that will do a good job on roses, too. Gaining in popularity each year is the hose-end sprayer. This is the type that is fastened on the nozzle end of the hose and as the water passes through the sprayer, the chemicals are mixed automatically. One of the advantages of this kind of sprayer is that the pressure is limited only by the pressure of your water. Also, it eliminates the mess of mixing.

The power sprayer should not be overlooked as a tool of the home gardener. Both electric- and gasoline-powered sprayers holding up to 20 or more gallons of mixed spray are available. You may think that 20 gallons of spray is a lot, but you will be surprised at the amount of spray material required for even a modest collection of roses.

In addition to a sprayer or duster, you might also consider having a pressure can (aerosol) of rose spray on hand. There are times when a little spot dab from the can is all that is necessary to kill some stray insects.

Figure 33 Two methods of applying insecticides and fungicides: spray (*left*) and dust (*right*).

CHEMICALS FOR DISEASES AND INSECT PESTS

The manufacturers of garden chemicals are making the job of insect and disease control easier every year. It is now possible to get from your garden store all-purpose rose insecticide-fungicide combinations. These mixtures contain the right materials to kill the most common rose insects and diseases. They come in both dust and spray form, and can be used in all types of applicators.

The common chemicals used to control rose diseases are calcium polysulfide (lime sulfur), sulfur, sulfur-copper, and phaltan.

Most insect pests that attack rose plants can be divided into two basic groups: 1) chewing or sucking insects, and 2) soft-bodied insects. The former type can be controlled with malathion in combination with other insecticides and miticides, while pyrethrum, diazinon, and rotenone are best on the latter. Except when a severe attack occurs, you can use a combination material formulated for roses that controls both diseases and insect pests. These formulas also usually contain a good spreader-sticker to hold the chemical on the leaves and stems. If not, add ¼ teaspoon of mild household detergent to a gallon of water for this purpose.

In recent years, a new group of chemicals called systemics have appeared in the insecticide field. Basically, they are insect poisons that the plant absorbs in its system; then, any sucking insects that take the juice out of the plant are killed. The effectiveness of the systemics ranges from four to six weeks. These insecticides are available as sprays and as granules that are worked into the soil. Systemics, however, will not kill chewing insects and have no effect on fungous diseases. There are some all-purpose sprays that combine systemics with other active ingredients for control of chewing insects as well as various diseases.

HEALTH PROGRAM TIPS

Regular spraying or dusting at intervals of a week or ten days is necessary for best results. It should begin with the unfurling of the leaf buds in the spring and continue until frost. Both upper and lower surfaces of the leaves should be covered thoroughly. The dusting must be done when the air is calm. Crank dusters provide a continuous cloud of dust and are very easy to use. If roses are being grown for exhibition purposes, the dust residue is undesirable. So use a spray. Other tips to keep in mind:

1. Special care should be exercised, in handling, mixing, and applying insecticides, not to inhale the dust, fumes, or vapors. If necessary, use a respirator that will protect the entire face. After working with insecticides, thoroughly wash the hands or any exposed parts of the body. Label plainly the containers in which these materials are kept or stored, and place them out of reach of irresponsible persons or children.

2. The general rule is to use the mildest spray that will do the job; read the instructions on the label carefully and make sure that you are spraying for the right insect pest.

3. Do not use any more spray than you have to; keep up the health of your rose bushes so that they will resist disease as fast as possible, and be on the alert for any setback.

4. Spray or dust early in the morning to avoid sunburn on wet leaves. In climates where the spray would dry in a rather short time, evening spraying or dusting may work out fairly well. This is a matter for trial and observation.

5. Usually it is best to irrigate your rose plants thoroughly the day before spraying or dusting, particularly when the soil is dry. Damp soil tends to prevent leaf burn.

6. Also, to lessen the possibility of leaf burn after spraying, shake or top off the surplus spray that has accumulated in cupped leaves and on the leaf points. An easy way of doing this is to use two light bamboo plant sticks approximately 5 feet long, held in one hand with the ends about 10 inches apart.

7. The ingredients used in some sprayers will, if left in the tank or jar, gum up or corrode metallic parts. It is a basic rule to rinse or clean them thoroughly after each use, drain them, and store them so that they will dry.

8. If you come upon a disease or insect pest problem that is out of the usual do not hesitate to contact your state college, your county agent, or the regional counsellor of the American Rose Society.

DISEASES AND THEIR CONTROL

Although hybridizers of roses have produced many new disease-resistant varieties, the home gardener still must protect his roses against the many diseases of roses. Fortunately, most of them are of minor importance—or appear chiefly on plants that have been weakened by unfavorable cultural conditions, unfavorable climatic factors, insects, or some other disease. It is true, however, that blackspot, powdery mildew, rust, crown gall, and the cankers may be considered to be of major importance. Furthermore, control measures commonly recommended for blackspot or powdery mildew are effective against rust, and frequently are indirectly effective in controlling the canker diseases.

BLACKSPOT

Blackspot disease takes its name from the small round blackish spots that it produces on rose leaflets, mainly observable on the upper surfaces. In addition, it causes a yellowing of the leaf area around the black spots, and the combined effect is early defoliation of the plant. With the loss of its leaves, a rose plant will not produce as many blossoms as it otherwise would, and the plant is likely to enter the winter season in a partially starved condition. The root system is usually meager in such plants and the amount of reserve food in both roots and tops so slight that, even if the plants survive the winter, the amount of initial growth is likely to be quite limited in the following spring. Plants infected with blackspot or otherwise weakened are predisposed to dieback and to stem cankers.

Blackspot is indirectly responsible for a pale flower color often occurring in many varieties. Diseased leaves and defoliated plants manufacture less of the sugars that are important in intensifying flower color.

The disease is caused by a fungous parasite that is largely disseminated by rain and which depends on moisture for penetration of rose leaf and stem tissue. Consequently, blackspot is most serious in areas of high rainfall and is least serious in arid regions. Even in dry regions, overhead irrigation may per-

Figure 34 One of the most common rose diseases: blackspot.

mit the development and spread of this disease when viable spores are present. Because blackspot is spread by splashing water, greenhouse operators no longer syringe their roses, and they spray for insect control during the morning of a bright day, so the foliage will dry rapidly. Aerosol bombs are now generally used in greenhouses to control insects and, as a consequence, blackspot of roses grown under glass has declined from the rank of disease enemy No. 1 to insignificance.

Free water must be present on rose leaves for at least 6 hours before blackspot infection will take place. With favorable moisture and temperature conditions, it takes seven to ten days for the typical radiate spots to appear.

All classes of roses are susceptible to blackspot in varying degrees. Roses of Austrian brier ancestry are especially susceptible, whereas those from *wichuraiana* and *rugosa* types are generally resistant. Polyanthas, grandifloras, teas, and hybrid teas are all susceptible. The Welch variety of multiflora understock is highly resistant, if not immune.

100

Control. The best control for blackspot—and *all* rose diseases—is sanitation. No spray or dust will be effective if the bush is constantly reinfected. Keep infected leaves picked off the plant and the ground and remove dead canes as they appear. Cut dead blooms promptly. In the winter as soon as the canes are bare (either naturally or because, as a careful gardener, you have picked them off) spray twice, two weeks apart, with a strong dormant spray, soaking the beds as well as the bushes. As soon as the leaf buds appear, begin spraying weekly with a good general-purpose spray.

Phaltan, a wettable powder, is excellent for chemical control of blackspot and mildew. Wettable sulfur sprays, with a good spreader-sticker added, are effective for both diseases, too. A good grade of dusting sulfur, a mixture of sulfur-lead arsenate (Massey dust), or a sulfur-copper dust (90:10) are all very effective. Copper sprays are very effective against blackspot but not against mildew. Copper may cause foliage injury at temperatures below 65 degrees F. Too frequent use of sulfur during dry, hot weather may result in burning the foliage.

POWDERY MILDEW

Powdery mildew is characterized by white powdery masses of spores on young leaves, shoots, and buds. These powdery masses occur as blister-like areas on young leaves. On the older leaves they appear as grayish-white patches.

On young shoots mildew may cause swellings or marked distortion. In severe attacks the foliage is stunted and the leaves and shoots are badly distorted. Unopened buds may be covered with the powdery masses of white spores. Late in the season the patches of white mold take on a dirty gray color, and minute, spherical black bodies may be seen embedded in them. These black bodies are the resting spore stage of the fungus, which enables it to survive the winter on persistent or fallen leaves and in infected bud scales and flower stems.

In contrast to blackspot, powdery mildew is not spread by too much water. The spores are wind-borne. In fact, excessive rainfall or syringing retards the development of powdery mildew. While the mycelium or vegetative body of the blackspot fungus grows within the leaf, the mycelium of the powdery mildew fungus grows almost entirely on the outside of the leaf and therefore

101

may be injured rather than spread by splashing water. Temperatures higher than 85 degrees F. are unfavorable for mildew development.

This disease can be severe in areas of low rainfall, because the humidity at the surface of young leaves is high enough to permit good germination of the disease spores even though atmospheric humidity is low. Under favorable temperature conditions only a few days need elapse after infection before numbers of spores are ready to be blown by gentle air currents to new leaves where many new infections will be established.

Hybrid teas, climbers, and rambler roses are usually considered highly susceptible to powdery mildew, whereas *wichuraiana* roses are regarded as very resistant.

Control. The same preventive program for the control of blackspot holds good for powdery mildew. In some areas, especially in the Western part of the United States, calcium polysulfide (lime sulfur) is most effective. This material makes a good dormant spray when mixed for this purpose, as directed by the maker.

RUST

The rust of roses is very destructive wherever it is found. It is favored by a cool, humid summer climate followed by mild winters. The Pacific Coast is the only large climatic region where these favorable temperature and moisture conditions regularly prevail.

The most characteristic symptom of this disease is the appearance of small orange-colored pustules. In early spring very small, inconspicuous orange or yellow masses may appear on either surface of the leaves. Later, the typical orange-colored pustules appear on the lower surface. Spores from these pustules may be blown to other leaves where they start new infections. In late summer or early fall the character of these pustules changes and black ones appear. The pustules that remain over winter within the leaf tissue after the leaves have fallen produce spores that cause the spring infection. Young green stems may also be infected, but the most serious injury is the defoliation that results from a severe attack.

Control. Employ the same basic program for fighting leaf rust as you do blackspot. In addition, acti-dione PM and karathane are good rust eradicants and can be used to control mildew, too.

ANTHRACNOSE

Anthracnose disease attacks both leaves and stems making small clusters of spots. The leaf spots are scattered or grouped, sometimes running together, usually circular, up to ¼ inch across. Young spots are red, varying to brown or dark purple on upper leaf surface, showing up two to six days after innoculation but not visible on the undersurface for two to four weeks, then dull reddish-brown to pale purple. On aging, the center of the spot turns ashen white, with a dark margin. Leaves may turn yellow or reddish around the spots, and may have slits or perforations as the centers fall out.

Cane spots are circular to elongated, raised, and brown or purple, with depressed light centers and dark fruiting bodies. The fungus winters in cane spots; spores are produced and spread only in rainy periods.

Control. The same preventive and spray or chemical dust program recommended for blackspot is advised for anthracnose control.

CANKER DISEASES

There are several canker diseases of roses—stem canker, crown canker, brown canker, and brand canker. In general cankers occur only in plants that have suffered wounds or in plants that have been weakened by causes such as excessive defoliation by blackspot, winter injury, or poor nutrition.

Cankers first appear as small, reddish spots on the stems. They grow in size and eventually encircle the stem. As they increase in size they become darker in color, changing from light to dark brown, and small fruiting bodies of the fungus appear within the discolored area. The bark in the infected area dries out and splits. If the cane is girdled by the canker, the leaves above the canker wilt and this portion of the cane will die. If the canker is allowed to remain, the disease may spread slowly down the cane and eventually kill the lower branches.

Control. Control of the canker diseases lies mainly in prevention. If the plants are maintained in a healthy condition, if wounds are avoided, if proper winter protection is provided, and if care is taken when pruning, the cankers, with the exception of brown canker, should be of little concern.

The danger of canker infections can be reduced when pruning, if clean cuts are made near a bud. Such cuts heal quickly. Ragged cuts and cuts made too far from a bud heal slowly and are vulnerable to attack by canker fungi. All cankered canes should be pruned out whenever detected. Special care should be taken in the late spring, just before growth begins, to detect and remove cankered canes. Disinfect shears and other cutting tools before each cut is made and after use on cankerous parts of the bush with a household disinfectant, rubbing alcohol, or a garden fungicide in order not to spread the infection. All infected parts should, of course, be burned.

CROWN GALL

Crown gall is a bacterial disease that affects many plants, including roses. The galls characteristic of the disease usually occur at the ground level, but may sometimes be found on the upper portion of the stem or on the roots. They begin as small swellings that slowly increase in size. Galls may become quite large before they produce any noticeable effect on the growth of the plant. Infected plants become stunted and eventually may be killed.

The organism causing the disease does not kill the plant tissue; it stimulates abnormal growth of the plant tissue that results in the formation of galls.

Control. The control of this disease is largely a matter of prevention. Buy plants free of crown gall and plant them in soil that has been free of crown-gall-infected plants for at least two years.

A plant once infected with crown gall cannot be cured. Infected plants should be removed and burned. The soil also should be removed in the vicinity of the infected plant and replaced with clean soil before planting a new rose in the same location.

CHLOROSIS

Yellowing of the leaves is often the result of poor drainage or unsatisfactory watering or possibly lack of light, but chlorosis, a physiological disorder, is more marked and serious than this. The loss of green coloring and part, or complete, yellowing of the leaf beginning with the young foliage tells the story.

Generally, chlorosis is due to iron deficiency and is quite common in the arid Southwest where the land has a high calcium carbonate content.

Control. This condition can generally by remedied by soil treatments, adding sulfur or iron sulfate at not more than 1 to 2 pounds per 100 square feet for a single application, followed by a mulch. For an immediate effect, spray foliage with iron sulfate, 1 ounce to 3 gallons of water. Chelated iron, sold under various trade names, may be applied to the soil to get a quick effect. Use on foliage with great caution, following directions for dilution. Avoid excessive irrigation with highly alkaline water.

VIRUS DISEASE

There are a number of virus diseases that attack roses. So far as we know, none of these diseases that occur in the United States is transmitted by insects. Characteristically, virus diseases transmitted by insects spread rapidly. In this country, viruses are carried in cuttings and scions taken from infected plants, and the spread of the diseases seems to occur only during propagation.

The symptoms of the rose viruses vary widely. The leaves of plants infected with mosaic have small, angular, chlorotic spots, which show a characteristic lack of color. They are most numerous at or near the midribs of the leaflets. Ring, oak-leaf, and watermark patterns can be observed at times. There may be no reduction in vigor or the plant may be slightly to severely dwarfed.

The "yellow mosaics" differ from the above mosaics mainly in color. The chlorotic areas generally are a brighter and lighter yellow, and very conspicuous. A third virus disease, known as rose streak, produces brown rings, brown or yellowish vein banding, and brownish or greenish ring markings in canes of climbers and others.

105

The development and maintenance of disease-free stock plants to supply cuttings for understock and the critical selection of budwood by the nurserymen should result in the production of virus-free roses. There is no evidence that the viruses of roses are transmitted by handling.

INSECT PESTS

Roses are attacked by a large number of insects. The most common ones are the rose chafer, Japanese beetle, rose leaf beetle, rose leaf-hopper, flower thrip, rose aphid, rose scale, rose midge, leaf-cutter bee, two-spotted spider mite, rose stem sawfly, raspberry cane borer, rose stem girdler, mossy rose gall, and rose root gall. Damage by insect pests is easy to spot. Laying their eggs where they will, they feed by biting the leaves and fruits of plants or by puncturing leaves and sucking the juices, and they infest the plant.

ROSE CHAFERS

Yellowish-brown beetles, known as rose chafers, are often abundant during June and early in July, especially in areas of light, sandy soil. They are about ½ inch long and have long, spiny legs. These beetles develop on roots of grasses and weeds and appear suddenly on rose petals where they feed and can destroy the entire flower. The rose chafer is difficult to control since it keeps swarming into the garden from surrounding areas and attacks the blossoms. Lead arsenate is unsatisfactory, and, although high concentrations of sevin and malathion or pyrethrum sprays will kill the beetles present at the time, they are quickly replaced by others. Hand-picking or jarring the beetles into a pan of kerosene is the most practical method.

Figure 35   Two of rose's worst flower destroyers: Japanese beetles *(left)* and rose aphids.

JAPANESE BEETLES

The Japanese beetle—about ½ inch long, bright shining green with bronze or reddish wing covers—causes a problem similar to that of the rose chafer, with the additional complication that the beetles destroy foliage as well as blossoms. Fortunately the main, spring bloom is over before the beetles emerge and there is time for a good fall bloom after most of the beetles have disappeared. During the height of the beetle season in July and August in heavily infested areas, it is impossible to completely protect the blossoms from injury. Many growers disbud or pinch off most of the blossom buds during this period to build up the plants for a heavier fall bloom. In areas of moderate infestation, the plants can be protected by frequent applications of spray containing sevin and malathion. In heavily infested areas the use of beetle traps and hand-picking may be necessary.

107

ROSE LEAF BEETLES

The rose leaf beetle is a small, oval, metallic-green beetle, which feeds in the buds and on the flowers of roses, often riddling them with holes. The insects are most numerous in suburban gardens near uncultivated fields, where the larvae feed on roots in the soil. The adults may be killed by dusting with multi-purpose dusts or by spraying with a sevin and malathion preparation.

ROSE SLUGS

Three species of sawflies, small wasplike insects, lay their eggs in rose foliage, and the dark-green larvae, known as slugs, feed on the leaves. Their injury is recognized by the skeletonized effect on the leaves. Rose slugs are readily killed by spray dusts containing sevin or rotenone-pyrethrum. The treatments must be applied promptly, because the insects appear suddenly and do their damage quickly.

ROSE LEAFHOPPERS

The rose leafhopper, a tiny greenish-yellow jumping insect, is frequently found on the under side of rose leaves. The insects suck out the contents of the leaf cells causing a stippling of the leaves that resembles injury by spider mites. Dusting or spraying the under side of the foliage with a contact insecticide will destroy the young nymphs and many of the adults. Systemics are also useful here.

FLOWER THRIPS

In many gardens the flower thrips greatly reduce the quality of rose blooms.

Figure 36 Insect pests that attack roses: *(top)* fuller rose beetles; *(bottom)* rose leafhoppers.

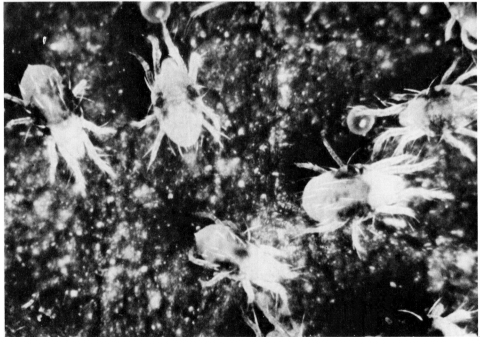

Figure 37   Insect pests: *(top)* thrips; *(bottom)* spider mites.

These tiny, slender-bodied insects enter the opening buds soon after they show color and, by rasping the tissues, they cause browning or other discoloration and distortion of the petals. Thrips can readily be detected by shaking the blossoms over a sheet of white paper. The flower thrip is a serious problem only under local or seasonal conditions favoring a heavy migration of thrips from the grasses, clover, and other plants on which they chiefly breed. Unfortunately, no fully satisfactory remedy is available because of the daily influx of thrips to the rapidly expanding flowers, which cannot be kept adequately covered with an insecticide. Applications of sevin and malathion in a dust or emulsion spray to flowers and buds every two or three days will destroy many thrips as they alight on the flowers. Systemics have proven to be very effective against flowers thrips, too.

APHIDS

Several species of aphids, but particularly the rose aphid, appear on stems, leaves, and buds of garden roses. By sucking the plant juices they stunt its growth. They often appear in large numbers on rose buds. The insects also secrete a sticky honeydew, which accumulates on the foliage. A spray containing sevin and malathion, diazinon, or pyrethrum and rotenone, and systemics are good in aphid control.

ROSE SCALES

Old rose stems sometimes become encrusted with white insects known as rose scale. The insects suck the sap from the plants; consequently, regular use of sevin and malathion dust during the summer will reduce the number of young rose scale crawlers. If the scales persist until fall, the stems most severely affected can be pruned out, and the remaining ones sprayed thoroughly during the *dormant* season with a white-oil emulsion containing malathion.

111

ROSE-MIDGES

The problem of rose midge control is complicated and no really satisfactory method has yet been found. The midge attacks new flower and leaf buds, causing them to turn brown and die. This tiny yellowish fly lays its eggs in the growing tips of the rose stems. The maggots that hatch from the eggs destroy the tender tissue, killing the tips and deforming the buds. The infested tips should be cut and burned to destroy the maggots. To prevent new infestations the egg-laying adults emerging from the soil can be destroyed by dusting or spraying the foliage with a sevin-malathion combination. Applications should be repeated every five to seven days for at least one month. Systemics work well against midges, too.

LEAF-CUTTER BEES

Leaf-cutter bees cut circular pieces from rose leaves and other plants, and store them as food for their young in burrows dug in the pith of rose stems. The tunneled stems usually die back for several inches. A carpet tack pushed into the end of the cut stems at pruning time will prevent the bees from entering and tunneling the stems. Tree-wound paint can also be applied to the cut stems.

RED-SPIDER MITES

The two-spotted spider mite sucks the juices from the leaves, which soon become stippled. As the injury progresses the leaves turn brown, curl, and drop off. When the mites are abundant they spin a web over the leaf surface. Infested plants are unthrifty. These spider mites are usually greenish with two brown spots, although some are dark red. They are almost too small to be seen without a magnifying glass. The spherical eggs have a glistening surface. The mites remain over winter as adults on leaves of living weeds or perennials. They become abundant in hot, dry weather. To control spider mites, clean up trash and living weeds in the early spring, and make frequent applications of a miticide such as tedion or malathion in a dust or spray. Make summer applications of either material at the dilution recommended on the container. A regular systemics program is also an excellent way to control the red-spider mite.

ROSE STEM BORERS

The stems of garden roses are occasionally infested with one of several kinds of borers, including the rose stem sawfly, the raspberry cane borer, and the rose stem girdler. These stems usually die back, and those infested with the stem girdler develop a marked swelling at the point of injury. Infested stems should be cut and burned. Applications of a sevin and malathion spray or dust at weekly intervals during June and July, when the adult beetles are present, will also help to prevent reinfestation.

ROSE GALLS

Several species of wasplike insects lay their eggs in stems of roses and their larvae cause large swellings or galls. One species makes a gall resembling fibrous moss on the stem. Another causes a large wartlike gall near the ground surface. The infested stems should be pruned to remove the galls and should be burned promptly to destroy the larvae in the galls before they emerge. These galls, formed by insects, can be confused with the crown galls caused by bacteria (described on page 104). However, if the insect galls are cut open, numerous larvae or the cells in which they develop will be visible. No insecticide known will control the insects that produce these galls.

Remember that sanitation is very important in the rose garden. Old foliage and weeds should be cleaned up because they become excellent sources of infestation by spider mites, thrips, and leafhoppers, as well as disease organisms. Rose chafers and rose leaf beetles breed in weedy areas or in other wasteland vegetation. It is essential to cut and burn infested rose stems having borers, insect and bacterial galls, cankers, and rose midge-infested tips. When pruning out infested parts, make the cuts close to nodes or buds so that they will heal rapidly (see page 118). In gardens where leaf-cutter bees enter the pith of cut stems, further injury can be prevented by pushing carpet tacks into the cut ends to close the wounds, or by painting the wounds with tree-wound paint.

ANIMAL PESTS

Rabbits, mice, rats, and moles sometimes will cause damage in your rose garden. The rodents will often chew on a rose plant during the cold, snowy weather when their natural food is scarce. Special rabbit repellent, available at hardware dealers, works fairly well, as does a wire fence. The rats and mice can be eliminated by *carefully* using poisoned bait of an approved commercial type where they can get it but other animals cannot.

While moles do not eat rose bushes, they dig tunnels through the garden and therefore may disturb the plant's root system. Special traps and poisoned baits are available to stop mole damage.

7

HOW TO PRUNE AND TRAIN ROSES

The pruning of roses, for some reason, is believed to be a very difficult operation, one upon which success or failure with roses depends. Actually, it is a rather simple procedure, but one which must be done with a purpose.

The main purposes of pruning roses are to improve the appearance of the plants, to remove dead wood, and to control the quantity and quality of flowers produced. If roses are not pruned, they soon grow into a bramble patch and the flowers are small and of poor quality. When pruning is done properly, the plant is not weakened, but if improperly done it may deform or destroy the bush. The methods of pruning should take into account the local soil and climatic conditions and the nature of the rose variety to be pruned. Bush, climbing, and tree roses require decidedly different methods of pruning. Within each of these groups, varieties differ in vigor and in growth and flowering habits. Pruning, especially severity of pruning, should be adjusted accordingly. With vigorous varieties, heavy pruning tends to encourage long flower stems and large blooms, and may be necessary to keep the plants within bounds. Less vigorous varieties, on the other hand, may be weakened and the bloom reduced in quantity and quality by severe pruning. All such differences must be taken into account in deciding on the best method of pruning.

PRUNING TOOLS

A pair of good pruning shears (or secateurs) should top the list of pruning tools for your roses. This is one tool that will be used from the time buds begin swelling in the spring until it is time to put the garden to bed in the fall. In fact, as your collection of roses grows, you may find it to your advantage to have pruners of different sizes.

There are two types of hand pruners used on roses. One of these—sometimes called the "professional" type—has a large single blade that has a slicing, scissorlike cutting action. The other, called the anvil pruner, also has a single blade, but it cuts against a piece of soft metal. The latter type is used a great deal by home gardeners because the leverage is greater and it is possible to cut a fairly thick stem with a minimum of effort.

Hand pruners come in several different sizes—the larger the size, the larger the stem it will cut. On ramblers, climbers, and shrub roses, though, you may have to use an even larger pruner, operated with two hands, called the lopper. With this tool you can cut branches up to an inch in diameter—just about the thickest you will ever encounter on your roses.

Another valuable tool is a pruning knife with its hooked blade. A good jacknife can also be used. Actually, some rosarians believe that the bulk of the pruning job should be done with it rather than the pruning shears. While complete knife pruning is more a method for experts, these rose people claim that it gives a clean cut, while the hooked lower jaw of the pruning shears bruises the side of the cane with which it is in contact. True, any type of shear will bruise the canes, if the blade becomes dull, or if the operator wiggles and twists the tool when it fails to cut fast and smooth for him. The remedy for this is to keep the blades sharp, and cut straight and smoothly, with a straight hand grip and no wiggling of hand or wrist—and if a cane is too large to be cut this way, saw it off instead. Keep the jaw below the cane and on the outside of your cut.

A small pruning saw comes in handy to cut out dead, thick canes, or canes that are too crowded to reach with the shears. In fact, one of the handiest saws for this type of pruning work is the blade of an ordinary keyhole saw. Around the upper end of the saw blade, wrap mechanic's tape to make a comfortable grip.

A can of tree-wound dressing or grafting paint—a black tarlike emulsion—

goes along with the cutting tools to paint the wounds made by pruning. Some of the new types are available as an aerosol spray.

You will also need a pair of leather gloves so that rose pruning is as painless as possible. Look for a pair that is reasonably well finished inside—the quickest way to get a blister is to have fingers working against seams while pruning.

WHEN SHOULD YOU PRUNE?

Pruning of established roses should be done *at least* once a year. But the exact time is usually determined by climatic conditions. Generally speaking, the common practice is to prune very late in the dormant season or just before growth starts. (This may vary from the early part of January in Southern states and Southern California to May in some of the Northern states.) Certain varieties of roses tend to die back when they are pruned too far in advance of the time that new growth starts, although many varieties will tolerate early pruning. If the work is done shortly before new growth pushes out, the pruning wounds will heal over in a minimum period of time with little danger to the plant.

Vigorous rose plants that have several flushes of growth during the season, like the climbing hybrid tea roses, which bloom over a long season, will tolerate cutting back twice, or even three times, if growing conditions are favorable. This encourages good blooming and maintains the proper shape of the plant. Pruning once in the dormant season and once after the first crop of flowers is past is a reasonable practice.

A few rose varieties flower only once a year, in the spring. These may be pruned just after the blooms begin to fade, thus insuring the production of the maximum number of flowers the next season.

The question sometimes arises as to how much pruning should be done after each crop of bloom is over. Faded flowers should be picked off. It is also a good practice to shorten in the new growth, cutting back to strong side buds or laterals. The uppermost buds will form new shoots that, in hybrid tea roses and certain other everblooming roses, will in time flower. After the second crop of flowers is through blooming, the growth may again be shortened in.

117

By this system, three crops of flowers can be produced under favorable conditions. When the regular dormant season arrives, the different flushes of growth made during the year are usually ignored. The total annual growth is rather severely cut back to a good side bud low down on the current season's growth, leaving only one to three buds on the growth made for the year, although occasionally more buds may be left on very vigorous roses.

Summer pruning involves the cutting back of vigorous new growth in general. Such pruning tends to be weakening, and should be limited largely to extremely vigorous rose varieties that need to have their length growth limited. The pillar roses also need some summer pruning to maintain a good shape when in flower. The totem-pole roses, or roses that have the canes woven about some form, should be trained during the summer months and perhaps shortened in occasionally to give the desired shape. Summer pruning should be limited mainly to this purpose, with no more pruning done than necessary.

As a rule, roses should not be pruned in fall, except to cut back any long canes that might whip about in winter winds and so gash or tear into the heart of the plant. Through the winter, roses subsist to a degree on carbohydrates stored in wood of the previous season. To cut this back severely, before cold weather, reduces chances of survival. Let major pruning wait until just before growth usually starts in spring.

GENERAL PRUNING PRINCIPLES

In making pruning cuts, you should keep certain general principles in mind. A sharp pair of pruning shears should always be used. Cuts should be made at an approximate 45 degree angle and should be made only ¼ of an inch beyond the bud or branch that is to be left, so that the wounds will heal over rapidly. If a longer stub is left, it will die back. No wound dressing is ordinarily required, although when a particular variety tends to show dieback after pruning, the wounds may be covered with a good wound dressing.

When deciding which parts of a rose bush to remove, remember that the canes can usually be expected to produce good flowers for at least four or five years and occasionally longer. Once a cane reaches the limit of good flower

118

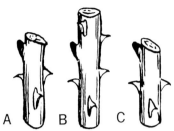

Figure 38 Basic pruning cut: (A) Correct cut, just ¼ inch above bud and same angle as bud. (B) Cut too far above bud and straight across, which promotes rot. (C) Cut too close to bud, which may result in injury to bud.

A   B   C

production, it should be removed entirely, cutting it back clear to the ground. New canes should have been developed in the meantime to replace the old ones as they are taken out. Rose bushes that are properly handled will develop new canes for this purpose. Many beginners ruthlessly remove all such new growth, perhaps in the belief that these new canes are suckers. Any new cane that appears above the bud union is potentially capable of making a good flowering cane in time if it is properly located and is vigorous. Very weak canes of small diameter or canes that are in the wrong position can be removed entirely, but enough canes should be left each year for replacement; that is, at least one good new cane should be left for each old cane that is removed.

Suckers that appear from below the bud union are another matter and should be removed entirely. However, to avoid suckering, most nurserymen remove all buds below the bud union when they prepare cuttings for rooting. Beginning rosarians often have trouble in deciding which is the sucker and which is the new growth. When in doubt, scratch away the soil from around the plant to check if the growth comes from the root of the bud union. The bud union looks like a gnarled knot if you compare it to the relatively smooth root. However, it is usually not so difficult to distinguish the old stock sucker from the hybrid rose. The sucker is *generally* a lighter green in color, has softer thorns, and has seven small leaflets, which are narrow. Suckers must not be confused with the strong basal shoots springing from the base of the plant—upon these depends the rejuvenation of the plant. That is, the basal shoots constitute the natural annual renewal of the cane growth and must be retained if the plant is to remain healthy.

On the other hand, once suckers start they will feed on the plant food first because they are below the level of the union from which the cultivated rose is growing. In short time these useless suckers will reduce a thriving hybrid rose to a weakly specimen. Thus, a sucker should be removed once it is *positively*

119

identified. To do so, trace the sucker back to its source, and gently take away the soil that covers that part of the original stock. Once you find where the sucker begins, it can usually be broken or pulled off the root. If the sucker is a large one with hardened wood, it may be necessary to remove part of the root along with the sucker. Keep in mind that if a sucker is cut or broken off at a point above where it originates, chances are very good that one or more new suckers will grow from the remaining bit.

It should also be remembered that when a rose cane is cut back to a bud or occasionally to a lateral, the uppermost bud or lateral will normally make the greatest length growth. This suggests the importance of cutting back to a bud or lateral pointing in the direction in which length growth is desired. In this way it is possible to regulate the shape of the rose bush: An upright one can be made more spreading by cutting back to outside buds or laterals, and a very spreading one can be made more upright by cutting back to inside buds or laterals.

But how far to cut back? There has been much discussion relative to this matter of long (high) pruning versus short (low) pruning or "whacking" of rose plants when giving the annual spring overhauling. While the argument still rages among rosarians, the consensus now seems to be that a high-pruned plant produces bigger and better blooms—and more of them—than a plant whacked close to the ground. Do not cut canes back to a point where the diameter is greater than that of a lead pencil, except for very good reason, such as when an aged plant must be reconditioned. If major surgery is indicated, cover the big cuts with a good tree-wound dressing to protect them. Remember that the protection of pruning wounds is important to prevent dieback, invasion of fungus infection, and entrance of borers into the stem system of your roses. Sanitary pruning tools are most important in rose work (see page 113). Blackspot, stem canker, and other fungous diseases easily can be transferred from a diseased plant to a healthy one on the pruning shears, and it is so transferred more frequently than many of us dream.

Whenever you cut blooms from your rose bush, you are actually pruning the plant. Properly done, it shapes the bush and usually increases the bloom crop. But, while it is natural to want to cut roses with long stems, it is not a good practice during the spring and early summer. The plants at this time are putting forth all their efforts to increase growth and flowers, and any unnecessary reduction of branches and foliage tends to upset the balance between top and root system. Insofar as hybrid teas, grandifloras, and floribunda roses are concerned, the vigor of the bushes will be much greater and the bloom more profuse if as

120

much foliage as possible is left on the plants. Later in the summer, when the bushes have reached maturity, cutting blooms and leaves will not matter so much.

Once the pruning job is completed, be sure that you clean up the entire rose garden. While doing the spring pruning, be sure to remove all leaves on your cut-back rose plants since these dead leaves can harbor and carry over fungus, diseases, and insect pests. Rake up old cuttings, leaves, and trash and burn them immediately. After your spring garden cleaning is finished, spray the pruned bushes and the ground about them with a 26 percent calcium polysulfide solution. Use at the proper dosage for a dormant spray. This spraying operation will kill any spores of blackspot, mildew, and rust on the plants, and insect pests wintering on or about the plants.

Bud-Rubbing

Bud-rubbing is a year-round supplement to pruning for control of undesired growth. It consists simply of keeping a sharp lookout for new growth buds breaking on the rose canes. If a bud appears that, from its position, you know will simply produce a branch that will not be useful and will eventually have to be cut away anyhow, rub it off with your thumb. This is actually carrying to the cane growth of the rose bush the same principle you apply to the bloom shoot when you disbud side buds so that the full vigor of the stem can go into producing a perfect exhibition rose. By rubbing off buds that obviously will not be useful in the growth economy of the plant, you conserve the plant's strength and greatly limit the amount of pruning otherwise necessary if such buds are allowed to go ahead and develop into cane and foliage.

PRUNING BUSH VARIETIES

Most of the modern bush roses are the hybrid teas, grandifloras, and floribundas.

121

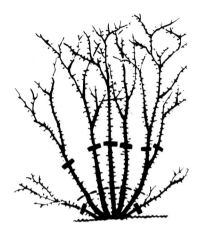

Figure 39 Bush roses are pruned in spring when leaf buds swell but growth has not begun. Basic principles are: 1. Remove all wood killed or injured over winter. 2. Remove all weak, twiggy growth. 3. Shape plants by cutting strong canes to a more or less uniform height. 4. If too many old canes, remove some at ground level. 5. Remove dead flowers in summer; always cut back to a 5-leaflet leaf.

They are pruned in early spring just before growth starts. First, the dead wood should be removed; be careful to cut an inch or so below the dark-colored areas. If no buds are left on the live wood, the entire branch or cane should be removed. Next, cut out all weak growth, and any canes or branches growing toward the center of the plant. If two branches cross one another, remove the weaker. Do not leave any stubs, but make the cut close to the cane or point from which it originated. Finally, shape the plant by cutting the strong canes to a uniform height, but leave as much good wood as possible. Cuts made on the cane should be just above a strong outward-facing bud.

There is no general agreement about how much should be cut back on a bush rose. Some rose fanciers prune to a height of 24 to 30 inches, while others prune back a little more severely, leaving the bush perhaps not more than 15 to 18 inches in height after pruning. The rose bush should be capable of producing long, healthy canes after pruning, so the amount of cutting back should be regulated to give these results. Sometimes a little heavier pruning will encourage longer new growth, whereas an unpruned rose bush will, in time, produce rather short growth. A reasonable amount of thinning out is desirable, to permit light and air to reach all of the buds. Also, generally, prune so that the center of the plant is kept open. Remove crossing or crowded growth and, wherever possible, take out old wood right down to the soil line. A well pruned bush should have three or four canes, evenly distributed at the base and tending *away* from the center. Clean the canes of all twiggy top growth. If there are small side growths, cut these off flush with the canes. To direct growth where you want it to go, cut just above an eye or leaf bud that points in the desired direction. In some sections, the winters are so severe that much of the top of the plant is killed. Under

122

these conditions it is not possible to do much toward shaping the plants. If possible, save all live wood, and be sure to make all cuts just above outward facing buds.

Certain hybrid tea varieties with brier blood seem to be weakened by severe cutting back. Such roses should not be pruned very heavily, and any large pruning wounds should be covered with a wound dressing.

Many of the polyanthas are upright and require less cutting back than most hybrid tea roses. Vigorous canes on these upright varieties may develop a cluster of roses, in which case the cane should be cut back to a sound bud just below the place where the cluster has been formed. To prevent the growth from becoming too compact, the canes should be cut to outside buds. The polyantha rose usually supports more canes than most of the hybrid tea roses.

Floribunda and grandiflora roses are variable in habit of growth, since they include both the large-flowered polyanthas and the low, compact-growing hybrid teas. Pruning of this class of roses should encourage a mass color effect for which the floribunda is valued. Only a limited amount of thinning out and cutting back is required, just enough to encourage the production of healthy flowering wood each season.

Figure 40   A floribunda unpruned *(left)* and properly pruned.

Most of the shrub roses should also be pruned after the blooming season. As a rule these plants are very hardy, so pruning is needed primarily to thin out and remove old canes. In all instances, this type of rose is most pleasing when allowed to develop its natural shape. A rose kept clipped to a formal shape is no more graceful and attractive than a forsythia or a spirea that has been given a crew haircut by some ignorant itinerant "landscape gardener."

Some types of shrub roses, such as *Rosa rugosa* and *Rosa spinosissima* and their hybrids, spread by surface or underground suckers and form clumps that soon become thickets. With these, it is necessary to do persistent pruning unless one secures plants that have been budded on some other stock. In planting these, of course, the union or knuckle should be kept well above the soil surface. There are others that do not spread but tend to grow taller year after year, becoming leggy and scraggly, with most of the blooms, in increasing numbers, borne at the tops of the plants. *Rosa hugonis* and that old but very worthwhile favorite, Harison's Yellow, which still is frequently to be seen in country dooryards or even around the abandoned ruins of old farmhouses, can be rejuvenated if the tall cane or canes are bent over and fastened down to induce the growth of vigorous new shoots from the base of the plant.

PRUNING CLIMBING VARIETIES

Pruning climbers is not at all the mystery it seems, and usually much less pruning is required than you think—but give yearly attention. Regularity is the thing to keep plants in bounds. Timing is always the same: Prune in very early spring to remove any obviously winterkilled or diseased wood; right after bloom to encourage the next crop on repeaters or to help train and keep a plant in place; at any time, if some growth is too rampant for the location and purpose of the plant. Grown as an espalier, a climber must be pruned on what is called the little-and-often system. Also at any time, you can remove suckers—growth arising from the root stock and below the bud or knob of the union. Usually a sucker has foliage noticeably different in coloring or shininess (though young leaves often look different from mature ones), and the thorns also may vary.

124

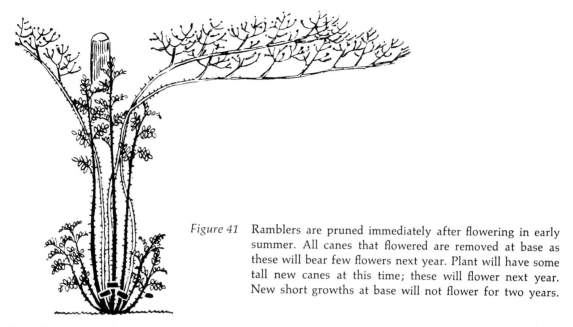

Figure 41 Ramblers are pruned immediately after flowering in early summer. All canes that flowered are removed at base as these will bear few flowers next year. Plant will have some tall new canes at this time; these will flower next year. New short growths at base will not flower for two years.

Seven leaflets are not a certain indication of a sucker, only the point of incidence on the stem.

Since climbers often require three years to produce a good flowering framework, prune lightly in the beginning and cut first flowers with very short stems. You should tend to train rather than cut a young plant. Tie the canes up or sidewise, according to the plant's nature. And study your plants. Some varieties produce only a few big basal canes from which arise many flowering laterals. Remove the basal canes only when they are crowded or cease to bear well, and then probably only one a season.

Most of the climbing hybrid tea roses have developed as mutations from bush roses. They will usually flower over a long period of time, and should be pruned moderately in the late dormant season. The side branches or laterals on the long canes should be cut back to stubs of from one to three buds. Most of the length growth of the main canes should be left, however. A sufficient number of new canes should be left to replace old canes as they are removed.

Pillar roses normally produce the best flowers on canes developed the preceding year. They may be pruned like the climbing hybrid teas, but the flowers are often better on canes of the past season. It is customary to cut out all canes over a year old. This annual heavy pruning encourages the production of many new canes. The new growth may need some thinning to prevent the plants from becoming too dense. Only the more promising new canes should be left.

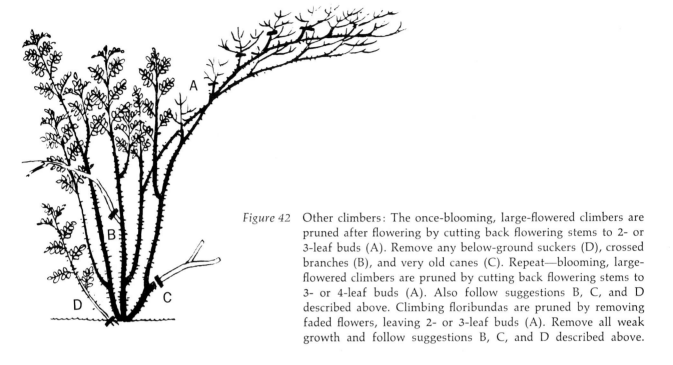

Figure 42 Other climbers: The once-blooming, large-flowered climbers are pruned after flowering by cutting back flowering stems to 2- or 3-leaf buds (A). Remove any below-ground suckers (D), crossed branches (B), and very old canes (C). Repeat—blooming, large-flowered climbers are pruned by cutting back flowering stems to 3- or 4-leaf buds (A). Also follow suggestions B, C, and D described above. Climbing floribundas are pruned by removing faded flowers, leaving 2- or 3-leaf buds (A). Remove all weak growth and follow suggestions B, C, and D described above.

The hardy rambler climbing roses should be pruned just after they have flowered. This will stimulate new cane growth, and the development of laterals on which the next year's flowers will be borne. Remove all old wood at this time so the plant can put all its efforts into the development of the new young shoots. Where the roses are trained over a trellis or any support so high that one season's growth will not cover it, some of the older shoots should be cut off at the ground, but the newer ones should be allowed to remain. Strong, vigorous canes should be shortened, so that laterals will develop and continue to elongate and eventually cover the supporting structure. In the spring, remove all dead and weak branches, but prune sparingly because wood removed at this time will reduce the number of flowers produced later.

Many of the large-flowered climbers, especially the everblooming types, do not produce as much growth each year as the hardier climbers. For this reason pruning must be less severe than on the ramblers and hardier climbers.

Remember, as a rule, that most climber roses require only a moderate pruning, especially during the first two or three years while they are getting established. If you wish to gather flowers during this period, cut clusters, not sprays, leaving at least two eyes on each stem. Long, arching sprays are wonderful for house decoration but each one you take sacrifices future bloom.

126

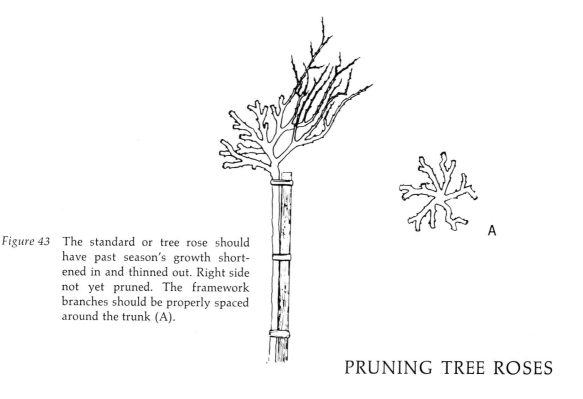

Figure 43 The standard or tree rose should have past season's growth shortened in and thinned out. Right side not yet pruned. The framework branches should be properly spaced around the trunk (A).

PRUNING TREE ROSES

Tree or standard roses are usually pruned to give a fountain effect. The ideal of most people who grow standard roses is a somewhat drooping habit of growth to give a rounded head and a satisfactory length of flower stem. They select their varieties with this ideal in mind. A variety like President Herbert Hoover is not suitable for this purpose. This variety, with its long, upright pole branches, is so unruly in its habit of growth that it can never be pruned to maintain the best form. Roses that are often unsatisfactory as bush roses, because of their tendency to produce curving stems, such as Debonair, Duchess of Athol, and The Chief, are often the most desirable as standard roses. If a wise selection is made in the beginning, less pruning of standard roses should be required.

The canes of tree roses should be cut back severely each year, leaving only one to three buds of the past season's growth. Only in this way can the head be maintained in the best flowering condition and with the best shape. It is usually desirable to cut back largely to outside buds, so that the head will give the desired fountain effect when in flower and so that the bloom will be reasonably compact. The pruning cuts should not be too evident after the plant is in flower, so it is especially important to make the cut close to the bud.

127

PRUNING OLD ROSE VARIETIES

Most of the so-called "old rose" varieties may be handled as you like. If you wish to prune to control size or encourage bushiness, the rules for general rose pruning hold, with only a few other points to be considered:

Once-blooming types, which flower lavishly over a long spring period and do not repeat, should have no pruning until after bloom, except to recondition an old plant. After bloom, a third of the top may be pruned off, and each lateral (side branch) shortened to three or four eyes. No more pruning, then, until after next year's bloom.

Moss roses can be pegged to cause more profuse flowering. By pegging, we mean that some of the long, willowy canes can be bent toward the ground in an arch and held that way with a string or wire, pegged to the ground. Or the plants may be trained to a fence. It is generally recommended that the mosses be pruned just after the first bloom and only once. If you wish to improve the appearance of a plant, at the general spring pruning time, cut to the ground any old or crossing branches.

Remontant or repeating varieties, of which you will find many in the old rose world, can be shaped and pruned through the summer as spent flowers are removed.

Tea roses usually have a weak habit of growth and require considerable shortening-in to insure more length growth and more vigor in the flowering wood that develops.

Hybrid perpetuals contain many of the remontant varieties that should give bursts of bloom. In spring, take off about one third of the canes' length. Also, if you have enough one-year-old growth, remove a few of the two- or three-year canes. We are told that hybrid perpetuals bloom best on year-old canes. Keep only the strongest laterals of last year, reduced on two or three eyes. During the growing season, reduce the new side shoots also to two or three eyes. Give these husky lovelies much more food and water than other roses and you will be amply rewarded by gorgeous bloom.

Bourbons should be treated like hybrid teas, previously discussed in this chapter.

Miniatures or baby roses. These little darlings, which are truly very minute forms of hybrid teas and floribundas, are pruned in exactly the same way as their standard-sized relatives. After a burst of bloom, moderate pruning just around outward-pointing eyes sets the tiny plants on the road to shapely form and their next blooming period.

TRAINING OF CLIMBING ROSES

Typical climbing roses, if given adequate support, grow higher and higher each year because the new wood starts from or near the top of the old. This habit of growth and stiffness of the canes makes them unadaptable for use as a ground cover. They are thought of primarily for their capacity to clamber over a trellis or up the side of a house on a support of some sort. If they are of sturdy growth they may be trained into bush form by proper pruning and staking.

There are various methods of supply support and, in this respect, the available material and ingenuity of the grower can be given full sway. A sturdy stake, or post, can be placed near the crown of the plant and a wagonwheel attached to the top of it through the hub. The canes are trained between the spokes, and the ends are clipped off when they reach the desired height. If a wheel is unobtainable, the same results may be had by fitting two pieces of wood

Figure 44   The easiest method of tying a rose to a fence.

inside a barrel hoop to serve as the spokes and a means of attaching it to the post. As an alternative, an X could be made of wood, and heavily insulated wire or rope strung from point to point of the X.

The height from the ground at which the wheel is to be placed will depend on the vigor of the variety and the preference of the grower. For vigorous varieties, about 5 feet is desirable. Tender and semi-tender varieties are quite amenable to this method of training as it is a simple matter to unfasten the wheel and lay the entire plant on the ground during the winter. The free circulation of air around the plant also prevents mildew, which unfortunately affects many of our most desirable climbing roses. When it is in bloom it is difficult to find a more attractive garden or lawn specimen and, at other times, the appearance is quite pleasing.

Four strong stakes placed close to the crown and radiating outward to about 3 feet apart at a height of 4 feet and braced with lighter wood is a method frequently used in England for training vigorous climbers. Suitable canes are trained up the stakes and tied together at the tips. Later growth is intertwined and the entire effect resembles that of a glorified balloon.

Pillar Roses. A pillar rose is best described as one that lacks the vigor of a climber and the wood is too short and stiff to ramble. However, it might also be said that any climber or rambler can be trained as a pillar rose and that this word should be used to describe the method of training rather than the type of rose. In either event, the variety must be suitable for the purpose of training about a post, or other support, in such a manner that all upright growth is encouraged. Horizontal growth is restrained by shortening all wood back to two or three eyes. The new growth that is produced by the remaining eyes is the blooming wood of the following season and, by pruning in this way, a pleasing formality and regularity in appearance are obtained. This training should be repeated after each blooming season and the older wood should be removed occasionally, at the base, to encourage new and vigorous growth.

To be effective and most attractive, a pillar rose (in fact, all climbing roses) should be clothed with foliage and bloom evenly from near the base to the top. If we were to study the blooming habits of the average climber, we would find that those shoots that grow practically straight upward bloom only near the top and that the lower buds remain dormant. Therefore, it is advisable, whatever the support may be, to train the canes so that they extend upward in a zigzag manner or, in other words, as nearly horizontal as possible.

130

Garlands of Roses. There are very few varieties of climbers, or ramblers, or pillars that cannot be used effectively if trained as garlands. In this method of training, posts are set about 10 feet apart and they extend 8 feet above the ground. Midway between each post a shorter one, about 5 feet in height, is set and a chain is draped from post to post. Varieties of roses that have soft pliable canes are probably the most suitable, and form the most graceful garlands. Vigorous growing types are planted at the base of the tall posts and less vigorous ones at the others. As they grow, the canes are wrapped around the post (one clockwise and another counter-clockwise) until they reach the top, and are then trained along the chain in both directions.

Rose Hedges. Any rose hedge, whether formed of bush roses or climbers, must be dependably hardy and of suitable growth. But no rose can be successfully made to form a stiff, formal hedge, and if such a hedge is desired the material should be boxwood, taxus, or privet, not roses. The greatest charm of the rose is in its gracefulness and bloom and both will be lost by "barbering." The rose produces its flower buds at points that would be sacrificed if the plant were clipped to produce a box-like effect. However, a certain amount of restrictive pruning is usually permissible and quite often necessary.

When planting a hedge of climbing roses, bear in mind that the hedge is to remain in the same spot for a long time and that repairs to the posts or wires, or the replacement of them, will become increasingly difficult as the plants increase in size. It is advisable, therefore, to choose a long lasting material for the posts. For this purpose, galvanized pipe of at least 1½-inch size can be employed.

To set the posts in place, first dig a narrow hole 30 to 60 inches deep and fill this with soft concrete. Then drive the pipe into the soft concrete and brace it to hold it in a perpendicular position until the concrete hardens. Finally, place a tin collar, to serve as a form, around the base of the post and fill this also with concrete, so that the concrete is brought up to 2 or 3 inches above the level of the surrounding soil. This last step is done to prevent rusting of the pipe at the ground level.

If a more rustic effect is desired, wooden posts may be used instead of the pipe. These should be of a wood known to be quite resistant to rot, such as oak, cypress, locust, or redwood. As an added precaution, they should be treated with a preservative material such as creosote, which serves the purpose well and is inexpensive.

The posts, whether of metal or wood, should not be spaced more than 10 feet apart and must be stiff and firm. Heavy galvanized wires, no lighter than ten gauge, should be drawn between the posts, horizontal with the ground, at about 1 foot apart. The wires should be wrapped securely around the end posts, which may need bracing, and should be as taut as possible. If the in-between posts are of wood, the wires may be attached to them with staples. If the posts are of steel pipe, holes should be drilled through them. If cost is of secondary importance, ⅜-inch pipe may be used instead of wire.

Wire netting, which is commonly used, is less satisfactory than horizontal wires, as the growth becomes entangled in the mesh and is difficult to remove when pruning.

Another very important matter to consider when planting a rose hedge is the preparation of the soil. Here, too, renewal is difficult, and for satisfactory long-term results it is advisable to spade the soil deeply and to incorporate into it a reasonable amount of peat moss or similar organic material. Chemical fertilizers can, of course, be worked into the top layer as needed, or a top dressing of manure can be applied, but the structure of the lower depths must have first consideration at planting time.

Climbing roses of vigorous growth habit should be planted about 8 feet apart and those of less vigorous growth somewhat closer. The distance between the plants, however, is dependent to some extent upon whether the hedge is to be a high or a low one. If it is to be high, say 8 or 10 feet, the plants should be somewhat closer than I have indicated, and the growth should be trained upward rather than semi-horizontal as would be the case in a 4- or 5-foot hedge.

The canes should be spread out fanlike and pruned quite severely at planting time so as to induce the production of new growth from the base of the plant. Subsequent pruning should consist of removing older wood each year. If the growth is permitted to become too dense, it will be difficult to manage and the plants will bloom less freely.

Ground Cover. Many varieties of ramblers are ideal as a ground cover and, like all other varieties having thin flexible canes, can be trained as a weeping standard, if attached to a post. The great majority of the ramblers are not at their best when planted against a wall, as the foliage is likely to become vermin-ridden and mildewed. A free circulation of air through and around the plant is beneficial. When used as a ground cover, the canes will usually take root wherever they come in contact with the soil and soon form a dense mat.

8

FALL AND WINTER CARE OF ROSES

All too often the rose catalogs use the word "hardy" to describe roses that are not capable of surviving the average Northern winter without careful protection. Quite likely this is why so many gardeners decide that they cannot grow them. They buy rose plants that are described as hardy, then the plants die the first winter, and so the conclusion is that in their area roses are "impossible." Of course, hardiness is a relative quality and varies considerably with location. Perhaps, therefore, we should not accuse the rose grower of intentional misrepresentation when he describes some variety as hardy that actually is hardy in a Northern locality *only when properly protected*. We do believe, though, that use of the words "hardy with protection" instead of the word "hardy" in such cases would ultimately increase the growing of roses in all our Northern states. Surely a brief note on how to protect roses by throwing a couple of shovels of soil over each plant would not discourage any rose lover from growing them, and certainly it would circumvent many a future disappointment.

The ability to withstand severe winter conditions depends on both inborn and external factors. The former are "in the variety" while the latter are influenced by the condition of the plant as winter approaches, the location in which it is planted, and the protection afforded it.

A rose bush may be compared to a hibernating animal that fattens during the late summer in preparation for a long winter sleep. The leaves are the fattening agent of the plant. Therefore, if we are to prevent severe winter injury, or

133

loss, we must be sure that the fall foliage is retained in good condition as long as possible.

Actually, the amount of cold a rose plant will withstand depends a great deal on the condition of the plant when it became dormant, and the manner in which the low temperature occurs. There is now some evidence that when roses have been protected against blackspot and other diseases, and thus pass through the growing season with their leaves in a vigorous, healthy condition, they are more likely to escape severe winter injury, since healthy plants are able to manufacture the maximum amount of sugars and to mature normally. When roses lose their leaves from disease or mineral deficiencies, new growth is usually stimulated late in the growing season. When this happens, the plants produce more leaves and go into the winter in an immature condition. They will, therefore, be more susceptible to cold injury than fully matured plants. One method of warding off winterkilling, therefore, is to keep the plants healthy and growing normally during the summer.

Another factor that influences the hardiness of a variety is the condition of the wood in the fall. If the autumn is dry and if cold weather approaches gradually, the chances of survival are greater than if there are heavy rainfall and warm days to cause late growth that will not have time to mature before severe weather sets in. Late summer feeding is also conducive to immature wood at the beginning of winter.

Briefly, then, early growth should be encouraged and late growth discouraged. Fertilizing, watering, heavy pruning, and cultivation stimulate growth. After July, therefore, the blooms should be cut with short stems, fertilizer should be withheld entirely, and watering and cultivation should be held to a minimum. If the bed has been mulched it will be found that both watering (except in extreme instances) and cultivation are unnecessary. Occasionally we hear of some rose varieties that are winter-hardy in one section of the country but suffer severe damage at a location much farther south, where the temperature is higher. Generally, the Southern location is one where the temperature is subject to considerable fluctuation throughout the winter. A fluctuating temperature in winter is far harder on roses than a constantly low temperature.

Atmospheric conditions can aggravate or lessen the effect of cold as registered by the thermometer. A long cold spell is more injurious than a short one, and continuous cold winds from the same direction are deadlier than "still" cold. Winter sun also causes considerable injury to the canes. It is therefore not safe to assume that the hardiness of a variety is to be measured by the mean temperature of the area in which it is grown. Snow covering plays an important part in

134

winter protection. A variety not hardy in an area where snowfall is normally light could quite possibly winter satisfactorily in a colder climate where heavy snows can be depended upon to cover the plant almost all winter. If roses are planted to the lee side of a hedge, away from the direction of the prevailing winds, the snow will drift in and increase the depth of the covering.

Adequate drainage of the rose bed is also important. Although roses like, and in fact demand, a considerable amount of moisture, they will not thrive during the summer nor survive the winter in a waterlogged soil.

Practically all the popular but tender hybrid tea roses can be wintered successfully in any part of the United States if the foregoing facts are recognized and adequate winter protection is given.

PROTECTION OF ROSES

In sections where winter conditions usually result in injury to the canes, it is necessary to provide some form of winter protection. There are many ways to winter-cover plants. Drifted snow is best but is rarely available when needed. Dry hay, pine needles, and leaves are often used as a top covering (not fresh manure), but beware of mice nesting in it and feeding on the canes. To discourage them, spray the roses and covering in fall with sulfur compounds, creolin, or even diluted creosote.

The safest and simplest method of guaranteeing survival is to cover each plant with a mound of earth after a few heavy frosts have ripened the wood. If additional insurance against winter injury is desired, the mounds, after they are frozen, may be covered with straw leaves, corn stalks, or any other material that will shade them and thereby prevent alternate thawing and freezing. For most hybrid teas, polyanthas, and hybrid polyanthas, as well as the so-called old roses, the best method is to mound up soil around the base of the plant and to stake and tie all canes that might be blown about, thereby loosening the root system. Pile the soil at least 8 to 10 inches high. In small rose beds, it is better to bring in soil from another part of the garden rather than risk the danger of exposing the roots. This protection should be given right after the first heavy killing frost and while the soil can still be easily worked. Inspect the plants

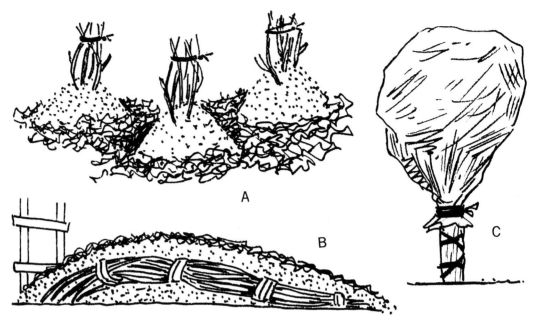

Figure 45 Protecting roses over winter is necessary in very cold areas. Bush roses (A) are protected by mounding soil over canes to a height of 12 or more inches after leaves have dropped. Climbing roses (B) are taken down from trellis, canes tied together and pegged on ground; they are covered with soil and then roofing paper, which is held down by stones. A tree rose can be treated in a similar fashion, or can be enclosed (C) in burlap with excelsior or oak leaves inside.

frequently to be sure the soil is not washed away before the ground freezes. Protection by mounding is usually effective in areas where the temperature does not drop below zero.

In regions where the temperature regularly goes below zero, protection in addition to mounding with soil is required. This may be provided by hay, straw, strawy manure, or leaves (oak preferred). These materials should be piled about the plants, and may be held in place by throwing on a few shovelfuls of soil. If evergreen boughs are available, place them over the bed, along with the soil, to hold the leaves or straw in place and to shade the earth mounds and roses from the sun. This will prevent any sudden change in temperature during a warm spell and will also protect the rose tips from strong winds. Modern floribunda roses as well as the grandifloras have more resistance to cold weather than hybrid teas. Hilling soil about the base of the plants is a safe precaution but usually a covering of leaves or other light litter will winter them successfully. When grown in small beds for garden effect, an easy way to protect them is to place side boards around the bed in the nature of a coldframe, filling the space between the plants with leaves or other litter.

136

Miniature roses, left in ground for winter, should be mounded over with sand or finely pulverized soil. In the spring those roses are pruned within an inch of the ground. Cut them again to the same height before bringing them into the house to flower (see page 140).

Tree roses and climbers are more difficult to protect in winter than hybrid teas and the bush types. In addition, tree roses are especially susceptible to winter injury and must be protected when the temperature is from 10 to 15 degrees F. below zero. These plants should be pulled over on one side and covered with soil. This is done by digging under the roots on one side until the plants can be pulled over without completely breaking all root connections with the soil. The entire plant is then covered with several inches of soil. An effective method in areas where the temperature does not often drop to zero is to wrap the head of the plant in straw and cover with burlap.

Climbing roses need protection in areas where the temperature drops below zero. The canes should be laid on the ground, held down with wire pins or notched stakes, and covered with several inches of soil. Even where winter temperatures are mild, protection from winter sun and drying winds is important, especially when the roses are growing in an exposed position.

Soil mounds should be removed as soon as danger of severe frost has passed. The soil must be removed carefully to avoid breaking off any shoots that may have started to grow beneath the soil mound. A stream of water from a hose is one of the best ways to wash the earth mound from between the rose stems. More of your tender buds will be preserved.

ROSES INDOORS

Roses may not be the "bloomingest" plant for the small greenhouse, but a few plants will give a great deal of pleasure. Variety selection is an important consideration. Commercially grown, indoor varieties are not generally available to the small grower, nor do they usually best serve his purpose. Where only a few plants are to be grown, many of the varieties that do well outdoors will be found satisfactory in the greenhouse.

Floribundas, as a class, are the best selection. They produce more blooms and do not grow as tall as the hybrid teas. If an individual specimen bloom is desired from a floribunda bush (which normally produces flowers in clusters), it is a simple matter to remove the side buds when they first appear. A few of the varieties that have been found satisfactory in the home greenhouse are: *Red*—Garnette, Red Pinocchio; *Pink*—Pink Bountiful; *Yellow*—Goldilocks, Tawny Gold; *Salmon-Pink*—Fashion, Pinocchio; *Orange*—Spartan; and *White* —Summer Snow.

Plants should be purchased as early in spring as possible. They are then potted in carefully prepared soil in a 8- to 10-inch pot. A good greenhouse soil high in organic matter will be satisfactory. The plants should be cut back to about 12 inches, and the pots plunged outdoors in the garden to the pot rims. Summer care consists of developing a well shaped plant by periodic pruning and keeping the plants free of insects and diseases. A heavy mulch is recommended to prevent drying during the hot months.

Bring plants indoors before frost. (Some growers prefer to wait until the plants have been defoliated by cold weather before bringing them indoors. It might be well worth it to try both systems and see which one is most satisfactory for you.) A night temperature of 60 degrees F. (70–75 degrees F. during the day) is preferable. Plants will grow in a cooler house but blooms will be fewer. They should have full sunlight—no shading at least until late spring. Give plants plenty of space on the bench, as roses need good air circulation to prevent mildew.

When cutting blooms, keep two points in mind. Leave at least two sets of 5-leaflet leaves above the hook (stub left from previous cut). The stage of maturity at which the bloom is cut is important, and experience will soon show the proper cutting stage. A too-tight bud will not always open properly, and one picked after it is well expanded will be short lived.

Generally, blossoms will last longer in water than when left on the plant, but if the color is wanted in the greenhouse it is perfectly all right to let the flower mature on the plant. For most roses, the time to cut is when the outer petals start to unfold, although a few varieties (particularly of the Talisman type) are cut in tight bud.

Care during the winter months will consist mostly of watering and feeding, as well as keeping a sharp eye out for insects and diseases. Roses should be kept quite moist, perhaps a little wetter than you normally keep other plants. However, soil must be well drained and water never allowed to stand in the pot for more than a minute or two. As frequent watering leaches out soil nutrients it is

Figure 46 Miniature roses make a good flowering plant for indoor gardens.

139

necessary to feed often. Use a liquid fertilizer every two weeks according to directions. It is important never to permit a rose plant to suffer for water or fertilizer; once growth is checked, many weeks will be lost in bringing the plant back into active growth.

Mildew is the most troublesome disease. Use care not to permit the foliage to be wet, especially on a cloudy day or at night. Give plants lots of room on the bench, as air circulation is important, but avoid drafts. If mildew should be noted, use a good recommended spray, preferably one that will not leave an unsightly residue.

Spider mite and aphids can be controlled with any of the good aerosol type sprayers manufactured specifically for this purpose. Use care not to point the sprayer directly at the plant, or injury may result. If you learn to discover these insects before the infestation is severe you will save a great deal of trouble.

As most small greenhouses cannot be kept cool enough during the summer for good rose production, it is best to plan on setting the plants outdoors in early spring. Prune back severely (to 12 inches) and plunge pots to the rim. With but little forethought, you can enjoy your roses all year if you are fortunate enough to own a greenhouse.

MINIATURE ROSES FOR WINTER FLOWERING

Many rosarians have known the charm of these dainty roses as grown in miniature gardens, in the foreground of perennial borders, or edging the rose garden, yet few realize that the wee roses, if given correct care, will flower indoors from late winter until time to set them outdoors again. And for those who have yet to grow these midgets, a novel and fascinating experience is in store for them. Miniature roses are exact replicas of larger roses but on an incredibly small scale. How any flower can be so tiny and yet so perfect is indeed a miracle. So small are these roses that a thimble or a vase less than two inches high will hold a dozen flowers and buds. The plant is very dwarf, and in proportion to the dainty flowers, with fine lace-like foliage.

For indoor flowering, or for winter bloom in the greenhouse, miniature roses are left outdoors for a period of rest in the fall and not brought indoors

140

until early January. A dormant period outdoors in the cold is a necessity before these roses will flower again. They may be brought in any time from early January on and should flower in seven or eight weeks. These plants may be purchased from nurserymen at the proper time for "forcing" in the house. The plants are potted in a mixture of good garden loam, peat, and a little dried manure.

After potting, the tops are cut off to within an inch or two of the ground, and the pots are set in a sunny window or sunporch and watered lightly but regularly. The soil should never be allowed to dry out. If the room is hot and dry, the plant may be covered for part of the day at least with an inverted glass bowl, thus conserving the moisture in foliage and soil. It is beneficial to lightly spray the foliage occasionally with cool water and to apply food in the form of one plant tablet to a 4-inch pot every three or four weeks. Rarely are these plants troubled with insects when grown in the house but, if such should be the case, they can be controlled by spraying or dusting with an all-purpose rose spray or dust.

Several varieties of "fairy" roses are available for winter flowering. Tom Thumb is a semi-double deep crimson with white at the base of the petals. The plants are quite small. Midget is very dwarf with small flat carmine red blossoms borne singly or in trusses. Oakington Ruby has a deep crimson bud, which opens into a double flower, also deep crimson with a white eye. The flower of this variety is slightly larger than the others mentioned, as it measures from 1 to 1½ inches across. Pixie, one of the most entrancing of all miniatures, is white in summer and faintest pink in the fall, or when grown in the house. After opening, the flowers will last a week or more on the plant and are long-lasting when cut. This is an ideal sort for miniature arrangements. A succession of buds is produced so the plant is constantly in flower. Baby Gold Star is prized for its luscious color—a rich golden yellow. This variety is much more delicate than the others and does not lend itself to indoor flowering as readily as some, but the lovely blooms are reward sufficient for any extra care involved.

Midget, while perfect in every detail, has buds no larger than a grain of wheat and flowers only ¾ inch across. Bright pink buds open into deep rose blooms. Rouletti is bright pink, vigorous, and long-lasting. Cinderella is white with velvety finish and at times a faint pink flush. Tinker Bell, well formed, many-petaled double, is bright pink. One of the most worthwhile miniature roses is Robin, blithe and pert as the bird of that name. This rose is fully double with as many as seventy-three little petals of rich, deep red. Tiny urn-shaped buds open into flat blooms no larger than a woman's thumbnail, the rolled and

141

curled petals giving a quilled look. These plants grow to 12 inches and have good green foliage with a smooth, leathery finish. Among other good varieties are the Dwarfking, deep red; Twinkles, white with slight fragrance; Baby Masquerade, cerise, yellow, and red, similar in coloring and appearance—except for size—to the floribunda rose Masquerade.

When miniature roses are seen flowering in the house they cause much comment because of their very minuteness and exquisite perfection. Their novelty and elflike bloom should prove a welcome diversion and uplift for the spirits of winter-weary gardeners.

9

PROPAGATION OF ROSES

Most amateur rose fanciers will find it more satisfactory and less expensive to buy their plants from a responsible nurseryman than to propagate them. A knowledge of how the work is done, however, may be useful in special cases, as, for example, in perpetuating favorite old varieties and others not readily available or in testing promising seedlings. Also, many persons find the work itself interesting and a source of pleasure. Patented varieties should *not* be propagated without permission of the patent owner.

Roses can be propagated by budding, layering, cutting, and seeds. The latter is a poor venture for the home gardener, unless he is interested in trying to produce new varieties of roses. Almost any of the other methods mentioned will get results in bloom far faster than growing from seed. Only species roses will come true from seed. If you try to grow roses from the seeds of hybrid roses, the offspring rarely resemble the parent.

PROPAGATION BY BUDDING

Hybrid teas and other similar classes of roses that bloom throughout the summer

143

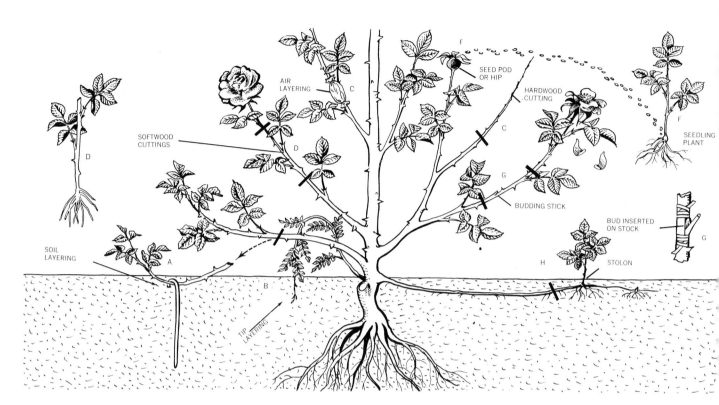

Figure 47 Methods of propagating roses: (A) SOIL LAYERING: wood near tip of lateral growth is partly severed, then pegged down and covered with soil. After roots form, new plant is severed from parent. (B) TIP LAYERING: tips of fairly firm new growth are pushed down into ground, where they form roots. (C) AIR LAYERING: firm new growth is cut part way through, surrounded with ball of moist moss held in place by airtight plastic wrap. When roots have formed in moss ball, stem is cut off just beneath it, and new plant is potted or set out. (D) SOFTWOOD CUTTINGS are taken from firm new growth, cut through or just below an eye, and treated as for hardwood cuttings. (E) HARDWOOD CUTTINGS are taken from dormant canes or laterals, placed in soil or rooting medium, and covered with glass or plastic film until new root system is well established. (F) BY SEED: parent varieties are "crossed," seed pods protected until well developed. These, when fully ripe, are gathered, processed, and later planted. (G) BY BUDDING: growth buds—at bases of leaves—are removed, and carefully shaped to fit into cuts made in bark on "stocks." (H) DIVISION: stolons (of some species) form roots and send up new shoots; merely need to be cut off and transplanted.

and are intended for garden planting are commonly propagated in either of two ways: 1) The cuttings may be rooted to develop plants called "own-root" roses; or 2) the desired varieties may be budded on to species that have been especially well suited to form root systems. Species used in the latter manner are termed "stocks."

Budding is really a form of grafting, whereby a single leaf bud, instead of a section of the stem, is taken to develop a new plant. Budded hybrid tea roses are usually preferred to those on their own roots for two reasons: (1) Larger plants can be produced in two seasons by budding than from cuttings; and (2) when well established on the best stocks, budded plants usually continue in more robust growth and produce more flowers than own-root plants of similar age under the same conditions. These two advantages more than offset the greater cost of production.

For field budding, one-year-old plants are used for understocks in most places, whether seedlings or cuttings. In the North, multiflora seedlings are commonly used. In the South, however, unrooted multiflora cuttings often are planted early in spring and budded the same season. The stocks are planted 8 to 10 inches apart in rows as early in the spring as the soil can be put in good condition. When seedlings are to be budded, they should be planted with the main root an inch or two above the ground level so that the bud can be inserted on the yellow root tissue rather than on the leaf-bearing portion of the stem. This low budding reduces sprouting from the understock after the plants are grown. A ridge of soil is brought up to the row to protect the stems from drying until they have started growth.

A very sharp knife is needed for budding—whether it be a pocket knife or a budding knife. Budding knives are made with a projection near the point on the back of the blade or with a flattened extension on the handle to use in lifting the bark. Such knives are needed if very much budding is to be done. Good work, however, can be accomplished with a pocket knife, if it is sharpened to a keen edge.

Budding can be done from about June 1 to September 15. The most favorable time depends on the condition of the stocks and of the plants from which the buds are taken. Stocks must be in a sufficiently active state of growth, when the bark will separate easily from the wood. This insures a close fit of the inserted bud against the wood that is exposed when the stock is opened. It is useless to bud if the bark on the stock has a stringy, dry appearance and adheres to the wood when an attempt is made to raise it.

145

The best size of stocks for budding have a diameter of about 3/16 to ⅜ of an inch at the point where the bud is to be placed. When the stocks are larger, the bark is correspondingly thicker. This additional thickness, together with the greater diameter, makes it difficult to bandage the bud firmly in place. Stocks smaller than 3/16 of an inch in diameter can be used successfully, but the buds are not so easily inserted as in those ranging within the limits of 3/16 to ⅜ of an inch.

The buds to be inserted are branch buds from stems carrying flowers at about the full-bloom stage. Such stems are commonly called bud sticks. The three or four buds below the flower (omitting the small bud next to the flower) are usually preferred to those farther down the stem because they are larger. The buds should be plump but dormant. A further indicator of the proper stage of bud development is the condition of the thorns. If the thorns separate readily without breaking the bark, the buds, at least part of them, are commonly usable. The buds of some varieties, however, break into growth before the thorns shed easily. In such instances, take the buds while the thorns are still immature, and remove the thorns by cutting rather than by breaking. Avoid injuring the bark while removing the thorns from the bud sticks. Next, cut off the leaves and leave only about ¼ of an inch of the petiole, which serves to protect the bud and assist in pushing it into place.

The bud sticks can be preserved in good condition for two to three days, if kept moist and cool. However, the buds can be injured beyond recovery in a short time if they are exposed to heat or dry air. Wet burlap, muslin, and water-absorbing paper are suitable materials in which to pack them temporarily. Some budders carry the bud sticks in a pail of water, taking out a stick at a time as used. The refreshener pan of household electric refrigerators is ideal for keeping budwood in good condition.

The stocks are prepared for budding by first drawing back any soil that may interfere with working around the stem. Next, prune canes that are so low as to be in the way. Then rub the stem free from adhering soil where the bud is to be placed. The side of the stock facing north is a slightly advantageous position for the bud, other things being equal, because it is shaded during the hottest part of the day. A matrix resembling a *T* in outline is formed by making two cuts through the bark with a knife. The first cut is vertical and about 1 inch long. A second cut is cross-cut near the upper end of the vertical cut to form the *T*. The bark is then lifted along both sides of the vertical cut by using the spur on the back of the budding knife or the spatula-shaped, reverse end of its handle.

146

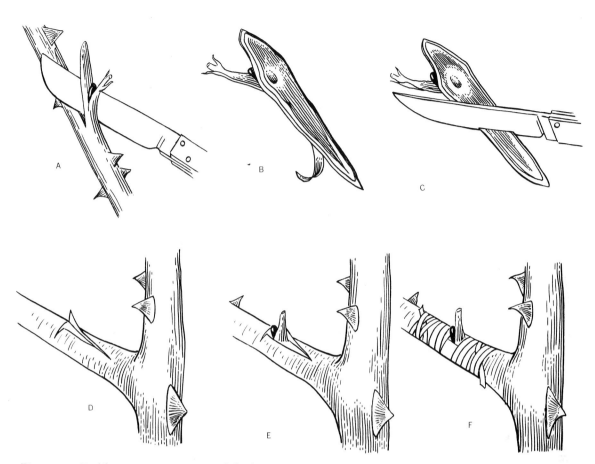

Figure 48 Budding a rose: (A) Growth bud, or eye (at base of leaf stem), of variety to be propagated is cut out with a long sliver of bark and wood attached. (Stem of leaf is left to serve as a handle.) (B) Sliver of wood is very carefully removed, leaving eye attached to the piece of bark, termed the "shield." (C) Base of the shield is then trimmed to a point, and cut off square just above the eye. (D) A T-shaped slit is made in the bark of the plant (known as the "stock") to which the bud is to be transferred. This incision should be in clean, live bark that will heal quickly. (E) The trimmed shield is inserted into the cut, until it fits snugly under the flaps of the cut and across the top. (F) The inserted bud is then bound firmly in place with a rubber band. When the stock is a one-year-old whip, the bud is usually placed at the base— the nearer the ground the better. It may, however, be placed higher up, or on a young lateral.

147

The bud is pared from the stem to include a shield-shaped piece of bark about ¾ of an inch long. Start the cut about ¼ of an inch down the stem from a bud, cutting upward, and run it under the bud deep enough to take only a thin sliver of wood. Some budders remove this sliver to obtain more contact between the bud and the inner bark when the bud is put into the stock. Others disregard the slivers of wood, but they are careful to include only a very small portion of it and to make the cut surface as nearly flat as possible so that the sliver will be pressed close against the exposed wood surface of the stock.

A definite procedure should be followed in inserting the bud into the T-opening. Start the bud into place while it lies on the knife blade. Then push it down with the thumb so that its cut surface is flat against the wood at all points. Be careful not to touch the cut surface of the bud. Also avoid folding the edges or tearing the flap of bark on the stock. The bud must be held firmly in place by a bandage made of twine, a strip of elastic rubber, raffia, or other material durable enough to last three or four weeks. Wrap the bandage around three or four times below the inserted bud as well as above it, leaving exposed only the bud or "eye." Keep the bark of the stock in place over the edges of the inserted bud while tying the bandage.

After two or three weeks the bandages should be examined, and, if the stocks have grown in circumference enough to cause constriction by the bandage, it should be cut on the side opposite the bud. It is not necessary to remove the cut bandage; it will fall away gradually of its own accord. When the bandages are cut, examine the buds and rebud any that have failed.

Ordinarily, buds remain dormant until the following spring, although occasionally one may start to grow within a few weeks after budding. In early spring when the inserted buds begin to grow, the stock tops should be cut off. Use a sharp shears or fine-toothed saw and make each cut ½ inch above the bud. During the first few weeks of active growth, remove any sprouts arising above or below the inserted bud. When the plants are 5 or 6 inches high, pinch out the growing point to encourage branching and to keep the plant low until the soft stem begins to harden. This precaution lessens the danger of the stem's being broken off by the wind at the point of union.

LAYERING

There are three ways of propagating roses by this method: 1) air layer; 2) tip layer; and 3) soil layer. The last is one of the easiest ways to propagate roses—especially the climbing types:

SOIL LAYERING

Choose one of the lower branches on the rose plant you wish to propagate. It must be long enough and flexible enough to bend down to the ground.

Make a slit or notch in the stem, far enough out from the central cane to make it possible to bring the slit down and peg it into the ground with a wooden peg or wire staple, leaving it still attached to the parent plant. Cover it with earth about 3 inches deep, and keep the soil moist until roots appear where the wound was made and buried. Use of the root-producing hormone powders, which are now available at practically every seed store, seems in most cases effective, though the plant will root without such treatment.

When the root system is able to take care of the shoot, cut the stem free from the parent root, leave the new plant in place until it is established—a matter of a few months—and then transplant to its own location in the garden.

TIP LAYERING

This method of layering is similar to the one just described, and is used generally for rambler class roses. When the new growth has become sufficiently ripened and hard—toward the end of the rose season—one or more tips, stripped of a few leaves, can be bent over and pushed into the soil to a depth of about six inches. The tip can be secured firmly in place by a short stake, driven well down into the ground. When the plants have become well rooted, the parent canes are cut off a foot or so above the ground and the following spring may be transplanted to their permanent locations.

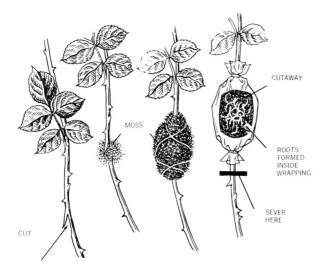

CUTAWAY

MOSS

ROOTS
FORMED
INSIDE
WRAPPING

CUT

SEVER
HERE

Figure 49 Procedure in the air-layering
method of propagation.

AIR LAYERING

This method—a modern application of an ancient Chinese technique—is easily accomplished and can be employed to propagate most classes of roses. As illustrated here, the leaves are removed from a section of a young cane or lateral; a clean, deep, slanting cut is made a half to two-thirds through the cane; and in this a little sphagnum moss is placed to hold it open. A generous wad of moist moss is then tied around the cane, and this is wrapped in prepared plastic film and securely fastened at the sides and ends. When the roots have formed in the moss, the stem is cut off, providing a fairly good-sized growing rose plant.

PROPAGATION BY CUTTING

Nearly all varieties of roses can be started from cuttings, although some root much more readily than others. The several classes of strong-growing pillar, climber, polyantha, and hybrid perpetuals in particular are often increased by this means, and the resulting plants are usually satisfactory. Hybrid teas and other similar classes of ever blooming roses, too, are very often started from cuttings. Ordinarily, however, they develop more slowly from cuttings than

150

when propagated by budding onto more robust types either while the plants are dormant or while in a state of active growth.

HARDWOOD OR DORMANT CUTTINGS

Hardwood or dormant cuttings are planted outdoors in the open ground in sections where the winters are mild. Such cuttings should be supplied with water during a long, cool spring season either by rainfall or by irrigation. Details of procedure vary in different localities, but the process for roses is similar to the general one followed in starting many other shrubs and trees from hardwood cuttings. The wood is taken during early winter while the plants are dormant but before the ground is severely frozen. Medium-sized canes of the preceding season's growth are selected. Avoid those that are extra large and any that appear immature. Until used, the canes must be stored in a manner to keep them fresh. Often they can be buried in moist sandy soil. Where damage from freezing does not occur, the canes can be taken in mid-winter. This wood is cut into lengths of six to eight inches at any time during winter. The cuttings are then tied into bundles of convenient size. Be careful to keep them all lying one way to insure planting with the buds pointing upward.

SOFTWOOD CUTTINGS

Home rose gardeners not interested in quantity production often wish to propagate a few rose plants of favorite varieties by softwood cuttings. One method often used is as follows: In midsummer, after the flowers have fallen, make 6- to 8-inch cuttings from the stems. Take off all leaves except one or two at the top. Then plant the cuttings firmly with half their length below ground. After watering, invert a glass fruit jar over them. Another way to make softwood cuttings is to take wood that has ripened well in autumn, remove all leaves, cut it into 8- or 10-inch lengths, and plant them in a well-protected sunny place, with only the top bud above ground. When freezing weather approaches, a mulch of litter several inches deep is put over them to keep the ground from freezing.

When propagating by the cutting method—either hardwood or softwood—it is generally wise to dip the base of each cutting in root-forming hormone powders to facilitate root formation.

STOLON CUTTINGS

Many species and sub species of roses extend themselves under ground by stolons, or underground runners, from which new canes spring up at intervals, steadily and gradually widening the area of the clump. Such roses, if they are not easily propagated from cuttings—and many are not—and if you do not wish to wait for plants from seed, can be propagated by digging down and cutting off a segment of the stolons with a shoot and some roots and planting them in a location of their own.

PROPAGATION FROM SEED

Reproduction of roses by seed is of primary importance to the breeder in his search for new roses with superior qualities. Seed is the principal source of new varieties, although sometimes new ones originate as bud variants or "sports."

Seedlings of the many garden varieties are of little value to the gardener who wishes his young plants to be like their seed parents, as such seedlings always differ from their parents in important respects and are usually inferior. In other words, as stated at the beginning of this chapter, the named varieties do not "come true" from seed. Nevertheless, some gardeners are becoming interested in trying to develop new varieties by means of hybridization. But, remember that even experienced plant breeders average approximately one commercially successful new variety out of five thousand seedlings that they have grown to a flowering stage.

To prepare a rose bud for cross-pollination, cut at the base of the petals. Then the emasculated flower has the pollen from the other plant applied with a camel's hair brush. Small curved scissors are excellent for cutting away the petals, and the pollen-bearing anthers before they shed their pollen. The emasculated flower is then covered with a paper bag to keep unwanted pollen from reaching the stigma. In a day or two the stigma is covered with a sticky substance called stigmatic fluid. It is now receptive. Remove the bag, and place the pollen collected from the desired parent plant on the stigma with a camel's hair brush. The paper bag is replaced, and, if the cross-pollination is successful, a seed pod soon starts to form. The information concerning the cross-pollination is recorded on a label that is fastened to the stem below the pollinated flower. All hybridizers place the name of the seed parent first in recoring a cross. Thus if Crimson Glory is crossed with Charlotte Armstrong, the label would read: "Crimson Glory X Charlotte Armstrong." The date the cross was made is also recorded.

True botanical species reproduce themselves within close limits of variability. Hence the species of roses desirable for use with other shrubs in ornamental plantings may often be grown from seed to good advantage, especially if facilities for handling cuttings, grafts, or other vegetative means of propagation are not convenient. Seedlings are grown in very large numbers, also, to form the root systems or stocks for budded roses.

When the rose seed pods (hips) appear mature, they are collected and the seed separated. If only a small quantity is to be grown, the seed can be taken out by hand. The seed of most species of roses is not in condition to germinate at once when removed from the plant at apparent maturity. It must remain for a period in a moist state at a cool temperature to complete the internal development known as after-ripening. A temperature of about 41 degrees F. is the most favorable for after-ripening of the seed of many species, although some germinate sooner if kept just above the freezing point. Storage near the coils of a household electric refrigerator will give approximately the correct temperature. The seed is usually "stratified" to keep it moist. Stratification is done by packing the seed in a box in alternate layers of about ½ inch of seed and 1 inch of sand or granulated peat. Peat is better than sand, probably because of its greater ability to hold moisture. The purpose of stratifying is to provide the seed with more even distribution of moisture, lessen the danger of heating, and reduce attacks of fungi that might damage the seed if kept in a mass.

The length of time required for after-ripening the seed varies greatly with the various species of roses. *Rosa multiflora* requires only a few weeks and germinates early the following spring. *Rosa canina, Rosa rugosa, Rosa hugonis,* and several other species are much slower. They require from four to six months under the most favorable conditions before they germinate. Temperatures that fluctuate between 32 and 50 degrees F. are effective for after-ripening, if the average is about 41 degrees. A longer period may be necessary if the tempera-

Figure 50   A hybridizer at work in his garden.

ture is not kept within narrow fluctuations. Under natural conditions, seeds of these species often lie dormant until the second spring after planting.

Crosses of varieties may germinate irregularly, some seed sprouting within a few weeks and other seed starting from time to time over a period of several months. Where it is desired in such crosses to get all the seedlings possible as well as species that after-ripen slowly, artificially controlled temperature is valuable. A household electric refrigerator can often be used effectively to provide a favorable temperature to hasten after-ripening of small lots. The seed should be mixed with sand or peat and kept moist. When the seed begins to germinate it must be planted without delay. Avoid deep plantings. About ¼ inch of sand or soil over the seed is enough when started under glass. Keep the soil moist at all times, but avoid overwatering.

If the seedlings are 4 to 6 inches tall, they may be left in the ground the first winter in areas where the temperature does not go below zero. A mound of soil, however, should be formed around them. Seedlings smaller than 4 inches are usually not able to stand very low temperatures. They should be dug and stored in a moist atmosphere at a temperature of about 35 to 38 degrees F. Such seedlings may be planted in the spring as soon as the last severe frost has occured and the soil is in condition.

154

10

MAKING THE MOST OF YOUR ROSES

The technique of growing roses is by no means an end in itself. Perfecting the methods is necessary in any hobby, if it is to be fully enjoyed. But, like most hobbies, rose growing has many other "side" benefits. For instance, you may have fun exhibiting roses in flower shows, or making your home more beautiful by creating attractive rose arrangements.

EXHIBITING ROSES

Exhibiting your roses in competition can be one of the pleasures of growing them. It is satisfying, indeed, to groom plants over a long period and then vie with your neighbors for a blue ribbon. In fact, showing roses places this hobby in the category of a sport, such as showing dogs, cats, or horses. As with any sport, showing roses *successfully* means following the rules of the show to the letter.

It is important to understand how roses are judged, what constitutes a perfect rose, what points of quality are considered, and what the judges look for. The judging of roses in the United States is governed by rules formulated by the American Rose Society. Rose shows have been conducted under its auspices for over seventy years.

In one respect roses are judged differently from many other flowers. The variety of rose is of prime importance, and each specimen is judged according to its approach to perfection for the particular variety. When there are several varieties in the same class, such as Crimson Glory, Poinsettia, etc., a judge must decide, "Is this specimen of Crimson Glory more nearly perfect than this one of Poinsettia?" or vice versa.

Because variety is stressed, all specimen blooms of roses must be named correctly. Visitors want to know the names of varieties they see; they may want to obtain the same roses for their own gardens. Rose judges disqualify blooms that are without labels or are incorrectly named, although sometimes a rose-show schedule will include a class for unnamed roses.

Every rose judge must know the characteristics of the different types of roses, such as hybrid teas, hybrid perpetuals, polyanthas, hybrid polyanthas, floribundas, and the various climbers. In many rose shows, there is a division of the hybrid tea varieties into decorative and exhibition types. The decorative type of hybrid tea includes varieties that are less regular or refined in form, even though they possess excellent garden qualities. The exhibition varieties have large, full-petaled, regular, high-centered blooms of ideal form.

The rules of the American Rose Society require that all specimens of hybrid teas and hybrid perpetual roses be disbudded. Disbudding means removing all secondary buds in the cluster and leaving only the main central one. Disbudding should be done as soon as the tiny buds are large enough to be pulled off easily. Other types such as polyanthas, floribundas, and climbers, grown for mass effect rather than individual blooms, need not be disbudded. While failure to disbud and late, or improper, disbudding do not disqualify a bloom, the presence of side buds penalizes it.

The scale of points by which roses are judged is as follows:

Form 25
Color 25
Substance 20
Stem and foliage 20
Size 10

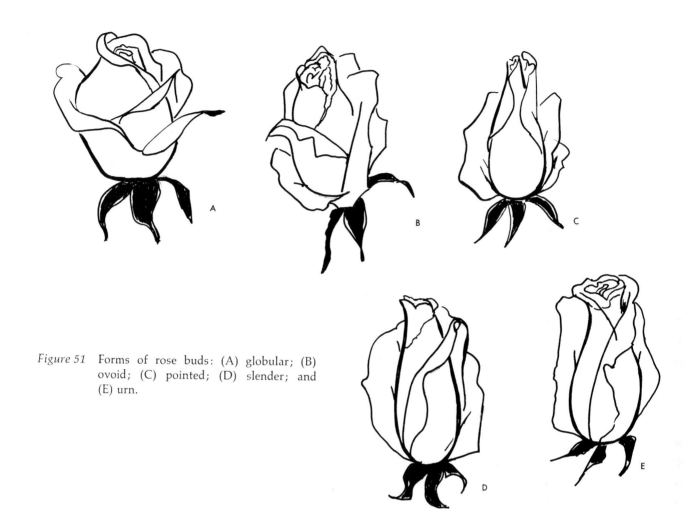

Figure 51 Forms of rose buds: (A) globular; (B) ovoid; (C) pointed; (D) slender; and (E) urn.

Form is usually the first thing a judge looks for. Form means the shape of the bloom and the arrangement of the petals. Ideal form is difficult to define. Symmetry is important; the center should be high and pointed; petals should be numerous and regularly arranged.

The stage of development affects form. At the time of judging, a specimen should be in the most perfect possible phase of its beauty. This depends upon the variety, but usually the bloom is half to three-quarters open. Buds one-third or less open do not qualify as blooms. Blooms not sufficiently opened to have reached their best stage and fully blown blooms are penalized.

157

A judge looks for defects in form, such as abnormalities or irregularities in petals, improper stage of development, split centers (not coming to a single high point), lack of circular outline, lack of symmetry, and poorly balanced arrangement of the petals.

Color is considered next. It should be typical of the variety at its best. It should be clear, bright, and luminous. Dull or blue tones and weak, faded, and washed-out colors are objectionable.

Substance refers to the firmness or crispness of the petals. Blooms should appear fresh and durable and should be of good lasting quality. A flower that wilts quickly and has very thin, limp petals is lacking in substance.

Stem and foliage should be in good proportion to the size of the flower. A large bloom on a short stem or a small bloom on a long stem is unattractive. The stem should be reasonably straight and stiff, and should hold the flower at an attractive angle. The leaves should be typical of the variety in size, shape, color, and texture. They should be abundant and appear healthy and vigorous. Injury from insects, disease, or burns, or conspicuous residue from sprays or dusts detract from the appearance of the stem and foliage, and penalize the flower accordingly.

Size of bloom counts less than other qualities in the scale of points. A large perfect specimen, of course, is preferable to a small one.

The clustered types of roses, grandifloras, polyanthas, floribundas, etc., are not disbudded but exhibited as clusters or trusses of flowers originating from a single stem. They should be at their most attractive stage. Some of the common defects are too few flowers open, faded and withered flowers, too few buds, and unattractive shape.

Climbers are judged by much the same standards as the clustered flower types. They should be exhibited as bloom laterals, which means a branch with a flower cluster from a main cane.

Every rose judge must be on the alert for errors in classification. If he finds a pink rose in a class calling for yellow varieties, he must disqualify it, because the exhibitor did not meet the specifications of the class. He must make sure that the correct number of blooms is present in classes calling for a specific number of specimens. If the class requires twelve blooms and the exhibitor has eleven or thirteen, the entry has to be disqualified. If the class calls for a particular variety such as Peace or Christopher Stone, the judge must make sure that every entry is of the proper variety.

Ordinarily, it is not easy for a judge to arrive at an accurate placement of the entries. He begins by eliminating the entries that show the most serious defects and are obviously not worthy of an award. Next, he tries to select the best rose for the first prize, and then proceeds to the second and third awards. A perfect rose is rarely found. Invariably, the judge sees some minor defects, and he must weigh one quality against another. If the competition is close, he should score each specimen according to the scale of points and give the first award to the entry with the highest score. His success as a judge depends upon how accurately he can evaluate entries in a class.

Rose judging is not an easy job. There are many pitfalls and opportunities to make mistakes. Failing to detect a misnamed specimen and overlooking a side bud on a rose that should have been disbudded are two common mistakes. It takes years of experience, both in growing roses and in judging them, to become a competent judge. Like a judge in a court of law, his duty is to interpret consistently and fairly the rules, which in the case of a rose show are the specifications in the schedule of classes and the regulations formulated by the American Rose Society.

THE ART OF ARRANGING ROSES

The rose is a first choice for indoor decoration just as it is a favorite flower for the garden. What other plant has blooms of such elegance and variety in form, texture, color and fragrance, and over so long a season, from late spring to hard freeze?

Finely sculptured hybrid teas arranged in traditional crystal or silver vases, saucy floribundas in copper or pottery containers, robust rose species in antique marble urns or fine china rose bowls—all have their own perfection. Roses also combine well with other plant materials and complement many types of containers. The old Dutch and Flemish artists, realizing this, often chose such arrangements as subjects for their paintings. We have seen yellow hybrid teas

159

expertly arranged with common bayberry in a pewter ewer; rich bicolored blooms combined with purple-beech foliage in a copper pitcher; roses, delphinium, snapdragons, and dianthus massed in modern glass or pottery; sweetheart roses with forget-me-nots in a child's flower basket; and fragile, single hybrid teas poised like butterflies, displayed in conch shells, and combined with lavender and statice. For the imaginative arranger there are limitless possibilities in combining roses with other materials.

Arranging garden roses is really simpler than making florists' roses look their best in bouquets. The finest greenhouse roses have perfectly straight, strong stems, often all but bare of foliage for many inches below the flowers. Although the blooms of these florists' roses are exquisite, the question is: What's to be done with all those naked, rigid stems? The obvious answer is to mass them in sufficient numbers to cover most of the stems, or combine them with other flowers and foliage in an arrangement emphasizing the rose blooms while masking their stems. Since greenhouse roses are cut as buds, all the blooms arrive in about the same stage of development; this makes the use of other flowers with them almost a "must." But with garden roses, even the beginner has little to worry about. Only the terminal buds of hybrid teas are produced on perfectly straight stems (and these are usually well clothed with leaves), while the stems of side blooms easily assume graceful curves. With a whole rose garden of your own to cut from you can select tight buds, half-opened flowers, and full-blown blossoms. Floribundas, grandifloras, climbers, and other cluster-flowered types almost arrange themselves.

No matter how simply they are arranged, roses are never plain. They fit into any container if their stems are cut in proportion to its size. Little vases work as well as large ones. Those with narrow tops are easiest to manage. Actually, the vases selected for roses should be only one third the size of the finished arrangement. If the vase you want to use seems too large, you can always add some other foliage for height, bringing the arrangement into proper proportions.

Glass, silver, or bronze containers suggest the places where they might be set in the house. Their shapes indicate whether they should be centered on a wall, table or used beside a picture. If you select the setting for an arrangement before you make it, you can let the flowers become a distinctive part of the room's decoration. A single rose placed in front of a mirror gives depth to a wall. The mirror reflects the stem and the leaves effectively without confusion.

While hybrid teas are at their best without other flowers, they may be used successfully in mixed compositions. Hybrid teas and climbers, large and small,

160

Figure 52 Steps in creating a simple, yet dramatic arrangement of pink hybrid teas. To start, set your "needle holder" in the bottom of your dish and fill two thirds with water. Add roses as shown, keeping stems in the water.

single and double, are effectively combined in the arrangement shown elsewhere in this chapter. Here the roses are mingled with delphinium in an old porcelain rose bowl to create a rich, fragrant mass of colorful bloom. Although it is not absolutely symmetrical, the bouquet gives the feeling of a symmetrical period piece.

Floribundas, grandifloras, or large-flowered polyanthas produce many blossoms on each flowering stem. If these are cut when only a few flowers are fully open and the rest are tightly budded or partially opened, there is no trick at all to arranging them pleasingly. Floribundas are the most suitable roses for softly rounded arrangement. They open in a spray at intervals, and you can cut off individual blooms as fresh ones develop. Generally, they are for informal arrangements and for masses of color. Sometimes a single cutting of a spray of floribundas can be put quickly into a small vase and provides an easy way to have cut roses.

The large-flowered climbers have a graceful elegance all their own, while the long, curving canes of new growth supply natural vertical and horizontal lines in arrangements.

Among the garden flowers that enhance the beauty of "Her Majesty, the Rose" are flowering shrubs, delphinium, stock, snapdragons, coral-bells, mignonette, *Salvia farinacea*, nicotiana, and penstemon for height, and poppies, dianthus, scabiosa, China asters, anemones, and chrysanthemums for rounded forms. A mixed tussie-mussie of fragrant old roses, pansies, dianthus, lavender, rose geranium, rosemary, and lemon verbena makes a delightfully scented and delicately colored bouquet for a dressing table or as a take-home gift for a parting guest.

One of the special pleasures of arranging is to know something about the names and history of your own varieties. Many guests will be interested when you point out to them that Eclipse has a long, characteristic bud, or that Peace is especially good in all stages of its development—from small bud to large, fully open flower.

Exhibiting roses takes two forms. Many garden clubs have classes and competitions for flower arrangers. Other clubs, including men's garden clubs, specialize in rose shows and in competitions for the most beautiful flower of a particular type. At various club meetings, you can get practice in arranging flowers, and the pleasure of meeting other people from whom you can learn.

As for imitation, people who like to be proud of their own achievements are sometimes wary of outright copying. This is a needless concern, if one eventually concentrates on originality. Rather, use copying as one of your beginner's tools.

162

Figure 53 Four attractive rose and flower arrangements.

For the first few times, follow good models—like the photographs shown here. Later, by watching a good arranger at work (as at a lecture) one learns principles, mechanics, and how to get ideas. Still later, instead of copying, the good arranger has learned to draw upon experience. As in any other art medium, the arrangement of roses can be used to capture a mood, to express meaningful ideas in a highly creative fashion, or to reflect, through the eyes and hands, your impression of a scene or landscape. Yellow roses can imply sand, a careful selection of reds can be used to illustrate fire, a bank of white roses may suggest a snow scene you once admired .

The tremendous range of possibilities in this special kind of "folk art" comes from the sheer variety of raw materials. The range of color in modern roses—from pink to brilliant red, from whites through every shade of yellow, from lavenders to bicolors—is alone enough to keep an arranger busy for years. The variations in containers, in settings and backgrounds, and in possible lighting effect add still more to the possibilities. Yet, the biggest variety is always in the arranger's own skill and interpretation. Incidentally, it usually is a good idea to grow roses whose colors go with your interior colors. If you collect copper, try the many orange-pink shades, such as Mojave. If you like silver, try the new lavender roses.

To obtain the longest-lasting roses, cut them after sundown, selecting partly opened blooms and buds that are just beginning to unfurl. Full-blown flowers make attractive bouquets for a day, but will fade within twenty-four hours. Cut the stems cleanly and sharply at an angle, and place in a deep jar of cool water to which the recommended quantity of a cut-flower preservative has been added. Do not crowd many roses together in one bucket, for the foliage may become tangled and the blooms may be injured when you try to separate them. Place the roses overnight in a cool dark cellar or shed, where the morning sun, which will open the buds wide before their time, cannot reach them. If for any reason you must cut roses in the heat of the day, place the stems at once in ice water and store them in a refrigerator.

By the way, if you buy florist roses in the winter, as home gardeners like to do, avoid bargains. Curbside stands usually sell cut flowers that are already several days old. Reputable florists sell fresh, well cared-for flowers. They last longer and make up for costing more.

When making an arrangement, handle each bloom with care to avoid bruising the delicate petals. The stems will probably need recutting to fit the dimensions of the design; the first cut is beneficial to the rose, for it permits the stem to take up more water.

164

If you want your arrangement to last, use a container that holds a sufficient amount of water. Add cut-flower preservative to the water and check the arrangement daily to see that the stems are well submerged. Do not place the vase of roses in a strong draft; it is particularly important in the summer to keep the arrangement away from direct sunlight. The cooler the flowers can be kept, the longer they will last. During the winter, when the house is being centrally heated, place the arrangement in a cool spot for the night. And remember, arranging roses is a delight, not a chore. It is a joy to handle the exquisite blooms and drink in their fragrance; it is a challenge to select just the right container for the color and texture of the flowers. Do not be bound by that old saw about silver and crystal containers being the only suitable ones for roses. Who says so? Use anything that you know will enhance the beauty of the roses.

CORSAGE MAKING

Florist shops carry roses twelve months of the year and send out countless corsages of them every day. For this purpose, though, garden roses are even more varied. The gardener who grows roses actually has several advantages over the florist. In a shop, most of the flowers are in the same stage of development and in a few standard colors only. The gardener, however, can walk outdoors and cut an assortment from tight buds to fully open flowers.

Roses most in demand for corsage material are of moderate size, glowing and long-lasting color, and fine form, and preferably with long, pointed buds. If they have the added virtue of fragrance, so much the better. Today, grandifloras and floribundas are almost as popular corsage roses as hybrid teas, especially with home gardeners.

Many other garden flowers combine well with roses. Forget-me-nots, astilbe, coral bells, valerian, and baby's-breath are only a few of the June perennials. During the summer, mignonette, verbena, cornflowers, candytuft, sweet alyssum, and such annuals are pleasing contrast. Also, if the variety of rose used for a corsage lacks fragrance, a spray of rosemary, scented-leaf geranium, lemon-verbena, or mignonette more than compensates, in addition to adding variety to the corsage.

Rose foliage is excellent for corsages. A lighter appearance can be given to large-flowered hybrid teas by wiring each bloom to one leaf. Contrasting foliage could be substituted for other flowers. The style of the corsage is also influenced by the choice of foliage. The shiny leaves of ivy geranium are somewhat stiff and tailored; small-leaved *Vinca minor* is appropriate with floribundas or rose buds, and feathery tips of asparagus or delicate maidenhair fern give a dainty effect.

Just as roses alone or in combination with other flowers or foliage set a style, so also do ribbons. Certain types of corsages do not need this added decoration. Satin ribbon complements elegant hybrid teas; dull textured grosgrain is suitable with certain kinds of foliage. Width, texture, and color must all be considered in selecting ribbon, if a bow is desired.

Roses should always be cut with a knife—not with scissors. It is essential to pick them the day before the corsage is to be made and worn. Evening is the best time, in order to avoid wilting.

After the flowers have been cut, thorns may be broken off or stripped off with a narrowly folded newspaper. Then the roses should be placed in a deep container of cold water. This is moved to a cool dim place, such as a cellar, for conditioning. Twelve hours are desirable. At corsage-making time, excess foliage is stripped off and stems cut to workable length.

The finished corsage will keep fresh if it is wrapped in cellophane or waxed paper and kept in a cool place. The refrigerator may be too cold. A temperature of about 45 degrees F. is ideal.

Roses—any corsage for that matter—should be worn with the flowers toward the face. There are two sensible reasons. Flowers naturally grow upward and therefore look better worn that way. Then, too, flowers are most flattering to the face.

In this "age of flowers," a man no longer considers it sissy to wear a flower in his buttonhole. It is also one way he can brag nonchalantly about the roses he grows, and it helps to start the day off right. Some men even have tiny lapel vases that hold water, and thus the rose can be worn straight through the day, instead of being discarded at lunch time. Lacking this, one should choose a rose bud at night, cut it off with a pocket knife, and put it in a glass of water until morning.

Figure 54   One of the best ways to learn about new roses and methods of laying out your own rose garden is to visit the various commercial and public rose gardens across our country. The one above is the Jackson and Perkins Gardens at Newark, New York.

POTPOURRI OF ROSES

Rose petals, combined with petals of other fragrant garden flowers, go into the potpourri, and not many years ago a living room was not completely furnished without this "rose jar" to add interest and charm. The potpourri mixture can also be used to fill sachets, and be placed in linen closets and lingerie drawers to give them pleasing fragrance.

One easy way to make potpourri is as follows: On trays, spread flowers (of several colors) of roses, pinks, mignonette, and heliotrope; any other sweet smelling flower; a few verbena; lavender and rosemary or thyme. Leave them in the sun for several days, turning them frequently to dry thoroughly. Bring them in at night. As they dry, place them in a deep jar in alternate layers with a small amount of orris root or unscented talcum powder and salt. Add a little allspice and powdered cloves. Keep them in the jar with a tight fitting cover for four weeks. Dried flowers of lavender, ¼ as much as rose petals, are also often used. Stir well and place them in a pottery or porcelain jar, and cover. A porous unglazed jar absorbs and retains the perfume for a long time.

Rose Petal Beads. Pick fresh, fragrant rose petals. Sprinkle the petals with salt, grind through the fine blade of a food chopper, and add food coloring or wall coloring to tint the beads. The beads will dry to a more intense color, so color lightly. For a red rose bead, use deep red petals and add a bit of red coloring, if desired, to make a brighter color. Put petals through a grinder several times after color is added to obtain a uniform blend.

Roll beads between the palms of your hands or on a board to shape them. Beads should be rolled about twice as large as you desire them finished, as they will dry to half size. Shape them carefully, to make beads of uniform size. Place them on a large platter so that the beads do not touch one another. Dry in sun. String them the next day after they have dried slightly.

String on a copper wire about the thickness of a darning needle. Do not sharpen end of wire or beads may split. Decorate them as you wish, such as indenting the sides or making impressions with the ends of cloves, and lay them in sun again to dry. When they are thoroughly dry, slip from the wire, put in a cloth sack, and rub gently together to polish them. Mix a few drops of rose oil with alcohol to "cut" it, and rub this over beads with hands, turning them over between your palms until oil is absorbed. When beads are dried thoroughly, soak them in olive or salad oil for several days. Wipe dry and string. They will always retain the perfume. Strings of rose beads can be twisted with strings of pearls for a more interesting color and texture effect.

Crystallized Rose Petals. Select highly scented fresh roses, dark red or bright pink preferably, and wash well. Drain on towel. Remove white pulpy base of petals, as this has a bitter flavor. Beat white of an egg to a foam. Dip small pastry brush, or fingers, in egg white and brush both sides of petal well. Or dip petal in egg white very carefully. Leave no surplus egg white on petal but be sure both sides are moist. Shake granulated sugar on both sides and place on tray to dry in refrigerator. They may be used for trimming cake or curled as a rosebud for a decorative garnish. When thoroughly dried, these can be stored in a covered glass jar.

Dried Rose Blossoms. This method of preparing roses for use in dried flower pictures is a quite popular hobby today. To accomplish it, select a single rose, or one without too many petals, and place it on absorbent, smooth paper. Spread the leaves and petals the way you want the finished product to appear. Do not use paper towels. The wrinkles will show when the flower is dried. Sprinkle with granulated boric acid. Do not use powdered, as it is too hard to brush off the finished product. Cover with a second piece of absorbent paper and put weight on top.

Let the rose stand for four days; do not look at it sooner. At the end of four days, carefully remove the top paper. This admits the necessary air to prevent the rose from mildewing. If the paper is damp, remove rose to fresh paper. Air and changing of the paper is necessary to prevent mildew. Flowers thus finished can be arranged in pictures and mounted behind glass, upon appropriate mats.

With these and other rose projects, remember that your friends will appreciate sharing your rose potpourri and other byproducts.

THE AMERICAN ROSE SOCIETY

In this book, we have made several references to the American Rose Society (ARS). This organization is the largest flower society in the country, with over 18,000 members. A national headquarters, full-time executive and editorial staff, and other solid assets for the furtherance of the rose offer many benefits to its members. For instance, the society's services include an annual survey of the newest and best varieties listed in pamphlet form and called *Proof of the Pudding*; a *Guide for Beginners* pamphlet; the *American Rose Annual*; and the monthly *American Rose Magazine*. The magazine carries articles written by amateurs and professional rose growers, as well as features on allied subjects, and includes news of rose activities both here and abroad. The society also maintains an extensive lending library containing the finest old and new books on roses.

Two national meetings are held a year, each lasting several days and including garden visits and rose shows. In these gardens and shows, practically *all* currently planted varieties, both old and new, can be found. At its shows the American Rose Society awards trophies and certificates to the best varieties in previously established classes. These awards, determined by the committee on prizes and awards, include the Nicholson Bowl, the M. S. Hershey Bowl, the Rosedale Bowl, and the Horace J. McFarland Trophy, while gold, silver and bronze certificates are awarded by local societies. All these awards serve to stimulate competition and recognize deserving gardeners.

While a professional staff conducts the daily affairs of the American Rose Society, the course of the various departments of program, activity, publications, membership, finance, and policies—everything that has to do with the management and development of the ARS—is charted and supervised by a board of directors. The directors are selected from and elected by the membership, and come from all parts of the United States and from all walks of economic and social life—in short, from the ranks of the country's amateur rose growers.

Application blanks for membership in the American Rose Society and information regarding its local branches can be obtained by writing to the society's headquarters at 4048 Roselea Place, Columbus, Ohio 43214.

Figure 55   Floribunda, Ivory Fashion.

GLOSSARY OF ROSE TERMS

The following are words, used in this book and *Home Garden* Magazine, that generally have a specific application to the growing of roses:

ACID SOIL.	A soil with a pH value below 7 (pH 7 is neutral).
ALKALINE SOIL.	A soil with a pH value above 7.
ANTHER.	The upper part of a stamen that holds the pollen.
APHIDS.	Small, soft-bodied, sucking insects. Same as *green flies* or *plant lice*.
ATTAR OF ROSES.	The pure extracted oil of rose blossoms used in the production of perfume.
BABY RAMBLER.	The common name for a polyantha type of rose.
BALLING.	The condition when a fully developed bud fails to open.
BARE ROOT.	A plant in a dormant stage which is dug up with no attempt to keep the roots covered with soil.
BASAL BREAK.	A new cane (stem) arising from budhead tissue or from a bud at the base of an old cane.
BASAL BUDS.	At base of the cane or at the budhead.
BASAL TISSUE.	The tissue or expanded ring of growth at the base of a cane where it connects with another cane or the budhead.
BED.	A level piece of ground in which the rose plants are set out in mass.
BEDDING ROSE.	Varieties of fairly bushy, uniform growth suitable for formal rose beds.
BICOLOR.	A rose with two colors or two tones of the same hue, usually one on the upper and one on the under side of the petals.
BLACKSPOT.	A fungous disease.
BLEND.	Two or more colors uniformly combined.

BLIND BUD.	All new rose canes are theoretically destined to terminate in a blossom. If they do not, the original "bud break" is called blind.
BLUING.	The tendency of some varieties, particularly reds, to become blue as they fade.
BRACT.	A small, irregular, leaflike organ found on stems between the flower and the true leaves.
BRANCH.	The stem or shoot arising from a rose cane.
BREAK.	The starting of any new stem or cane growth from a bud.
BROWN CANKER.	A fungous disease.
BUD.	An underdeveloped flower, shoot, or leaf protruding from the stem of a plant.
BUDDING.	A method of grafting a bud or eye to the rootstock.
BUDHEAD.	The enlarged expanded growth (from a single bud) just above the crown where the hybrid (or different) variety of rose was placed (grafted).
BUD MUTATION.	A sport or change that nature produces.
BUD UNION.	The suture line or point where the hybrid budhead was united with the rootstock.
BUSH ROSE.	A rose that produces canes that are upright in character and are in a bush form.
CALYX.	The outer circle of a flower, composed of sepals, which are green in a rose.
CANE.	The stem on a rose plant, has buds, nodes, hollow or pithy center, bears leaves, flowers, fruits (hips).
CANE HEAD.	An enlarged or spreading growth from a single thickened node on a stem resulting in a growth pattern above the budhead.
CANKER.	A fungous disease.
CHEWING INSECT.	An insect that eats holes in leaves, stems, or flowers.
CHLOROSIS.	A yellowing of the foliage.
CLIMBER.	A rose that produces long, flexible canes that require support to grow upright.
CORKY LAYER.	The corky tissue which extends beyond the skin of a cane forming a thick, spongy layer over the outside of the stem.
CROSS.	The result when two plants are cross-pollinated.
CROSS CANES.	Canes or twigs which grow at angles so that they cross other and larger canes and abrade, shade, or otherwise interfere with their growth.

CROSS-POLLINATION. The act of placing the pollen of one variety of rose on the stigmas of another.

CROWN. Where roots and stems join. An expanded and enlarged area which is more stem in character than root.

CROWN GALL. A disease that attacks the crown or budhead of a rose plant causing huge masses of bulbous growth somewhat corky, and with small, thin roots attached.

CUTTING. A piece of stem used for propagation. Also the taking of blossoms or flowers.

DECORATIVE VARIETY. A rose adapted for garden display but lacking excellence of bloom for exhibition.

DEFOLIATION. Loss or removal of leaves.

DEFORMED CANES. Canes, new or old, that twist, bend, or loop unnaturally or without purposeful training.

DIEBACK. The dying back of the cane ends.

DISBUDDING. Removing unwanted buds from the plant. This is usually done to make remaining buds develop into larger flowers.

DISEASED CANES. Canes, new or old, that show evidence of disease, such as cracked bark, skin breaks, bulges.

DOG-LEG. The replacement cane or stem that grows outward, then upward from a bud (or buds on either side) below the hat-rack.

DORMANT. The state of inactive growth, or resting; the state of lacking flowers and foliage during winter.

DOUBLE BLOOMS. Blooms usually possessing eighteen to thirty petals.

EMASCULATION. The removal of stamens before the shedding of pollen.

EVERBLOOMING. The successive production of flowers throughout summer and fall until frost.

EXHIBITION VARIETY. A rose capable of producing blooms conforming to standards of perfection.

EYE. An undeveloped bud, either leaf or flower.

FIBROUS ROOTS. Small secondary roots; hair roots.

FLORIBUNDA. A bush rose characterized by clusters of single or double flowers produced from June until autumn frost.

FLORIFEROUS. The quality of being free-flowering.

FORCE. To encourage rapid or early growth by means of

artificial stimulation, such as growing under glass in a greenhouse.

FORKED TERMINAL. End of pruned cane having two smaller canes at its top, extending in opposite directions, from one or more joints.

FULL-PETALLED. A rose possessing over thirty petals.

GRAFTING. A method of propagation whereby a piece of one plant is induced to unite and grow on another.

GRANDIFLORA. A bush rose characterized by large flowers borne singly or in clusters on stems long enough for cutting.

HAIR ROOTS. Very fine, hairlike, feeding or absorbing roots.

HARDINESS. The characteristic of a plant that enables it to live through severe climatic conditions, especially freezing temperatures.

HAT-RACK. The dead end or stub of a cane cut between buds (nodes) or above stem joints.

HEAVY SOIL. Densely composed soil, such as clay or silt.

HEELING-IN. Planting temporarily until permanent planting can be undertaken, should the roses arrive during unfavorable weather or the beds be unready to receive them. If the roots are carefully covered with soil, the roses will come to no harm for several weeks.

HILL UP. To heap soil around the stems of a rose bush, in a small hill. Same as *mounding*.

HIP. The ripened fruit of a rose, containing seed.

HUE. A color; one of the colors of the spectrum: violet, blue, green, yellow, orange, and red.

HUMUS. Thoroughly decomposed organic or once-living material.

HYBRID. The plant that results when two different varieties or species of plants are crossed.

HYBRID BUDHEAD. The growth or budhead where a hybrid variety of rose has been budded to a rootstock of a lesser variety, seedling, or species rose plant.

HYBRID PERPETUAL. A bush rose characterized by sturdy, vertical stems and attractive blooms.

HYBRID TEA. A bush rose characterized by handsome bloom, produced from May or June and thereafter regularly until autumn frost.

INFLORESCENCE. A cluster of flowers on one stem.

176

INORGANIC.	Matter whose origin is mineral, as opposed to vegetable and animal tissue.
INTERNODE.	Stem space between two nodes or buds. Has no regenerative tissue.
JOINTED TERMINAL.	End of pruned cane having a smaller cane attached to it by a joint and continuing away on an angle.
LATENT BUD.	A bud which is found on older canes but may be obscured by corky tissue, stubs, or debris.
LATERAL.	A short side stem growing out from a main branch.
LATERAL BUD.	A bud on a side of a node or cane usually pointed upward at an angle.
LEAF SCAR.	A line extending around the cane (partially at least) and thickened just under the bud at the node of a stem.
LIGHT SOIL.	Porous soil composed of larger particles as in loamy or sandy soils.
MAIDEN PLANT.	A rose bush the first year after budding.
MINIATURE ROSE.	A small plant, 6 to 12 inches tall, with foliage and flowers in scale to height.
MULCH.	Any material that, when placed on the surface of the soil at or near plants, prevents surface moisture loss, acts as a sponge for soluble fertilizing nutrients, and controls weed growth. It may or may not be a fertilizer in and of itself (as manure).
MULTICOLOR.	A rose with several colors or hues.
NEMATODES.	Microscopic worms attacking the roots of plants and causing small, knotlike swellings.
NEUTRAL SOIL.	Neither acid nor alkaline; pH 7.
NEW CANES.	New shoots or stems arising from buds on crowns, stems, etc. They have skin for outside covering, are green, brown, or red in coloring, and may or may not have discoloring in spots or patches.
NITRIFICATION.	The process whereby nitrogen is liberated in the soil.
NODE.	Thickened areas on canes at which buds appear and from which all replacement growth arises. Same as *joint*.
NOISETTE.	A group of rose varieties.
OLD CANES.	Canes usually one season or year (or more) in age. They are brown or gray in color, and show corky streaks and thickened nodes.

ORGANIC. — Matter whose origin is living tissue; decaying or decomposed vegetative and animal matter.

OVARY. — The seed vessel.

OWN-ROOT. — A plant growing on or from its own roots; one that is not budded or grafted.

PATTERN FORMATION. — All rose plants should be pruned to a definite design, pattern, or plan. Whatever pruning is done dominates the pattern the replacement growth will assume.

PEDICEL. — The short section of stem between the flower and the uppermost leaf; the neck.

PEG. — To fasten the long stem of a climber or shrub rose with a clothespin, if to soil; or with some other device, if to a wall or hard surface.

PETALOID. — Small, irregular petals in the center of double blooms, often showing the transition from anthers to petals.

PETIOLE. — The stem of a leaf.

PILLAR ROSE. — A slow climber; a climber trained on a post.

PINCHING. — The removal of the bud or growing tip of a cane to induce branching or formation of larger flowers.

PLETHORA. — The superabundance of small, undersized, low quality buds found crowded on twigs at top of rose cane that was insufficiently groomed or where careless bloom cutting has been practiced.

POLYANTHA. — A bush rose characterized by clusters of small blossoms, produced continuously.

PROPAGATE. — To increase or multiple the number of plants.

RAMBLER. — A climbing rose characterized by clusters of small blossoms produced only once a year, in June or July.

REMONTANT. — Blooming more than once during a season. Same as *recurrent*.

REPLACEMENT. — The cane growth from a bud which takes the place or fills the area of a removed, old, or lower cane.

REVERSION. — The taking over by suckers from the understock of a plant on which the bud or graft has dried out.

ROOT. — That part of the plant that extends underground from the crown. Roots are different in color, texture, and appearance than other parts.

ROOT CONNECTIONS.	Root attachment to crown, or to larger roots.
ROOT KNOT.	An injury caused by nematodes.
ROOT ROT.	Any number of diseases that destroy the root tissue at or near the soil surface.
ROOTSTOCK.	The seedling or "wild" plant species that was rooted from a cutting and on which the hybrid was budded. Same as *understock*.
SCION.	The leaf or eyes of the cultivated variety used for budding, or any bud separated from its parent and grafted to another plant.
SEEDLING.	A rose raised from seed.
SELFING.	The pollination of a bloom with its own pollen; self-pollination.
SEMI-DOUBLE.	Blooms possessing more than five but not more than eighteen petals.
SHADE.	The dark tones of a hue.
SHRUB ROSE.	A many-stemmed rose bush that can be upright, fountain- or mound-shaped in habit of growth. Mostly single flowers, often small, and appearing only once a year.
SINGLE-FLOWERED.	A bloom generally possessing one row of five petals.
SINKAGE.	The tendency of the rose plant to sink below the surface of the soil so that crown, rootstock, and budhead are all below soil's surface.
SNAG.	An unwanted stump, often the result of unsatisfactory pruning.
SPECIES.	A group of roses that possess in common one or more distinctive and constant characteristics.
SPECIMEN.	A rose grown by itself for effective display.
SPORT.	A freak of nature or any variation from the normal, usually a flower making a sudden appearance on a stem differing in color from that of the plant that produced it.
SPORT CLIMBER.	A sport that appears unheralded, with climbing characteristics, on a bush rose.
STAKE.	To support a rose plant by tying its stem to a length of wood anchored in the ground alongside.
STAMEN.	The male organ of the flower made up of a thin stalk and a head known as the anther. It is the anther which is the pollen-bearing organ.
STEM.	The branch that supports the flower.

STIGMA.	The end of the pistil or female organ on which the pollen is retained.
STOCK.	The rooted portion of a plant in which a bud is inserted to form a new plant.
STRIATIONS.	Streaks or lines of corky tissue on older or mature canes, indicate blooming capacity is nearly ended.
STUB.	The remains of a cane that has been removed, leaving its basal attachment to the mother cane and a short part of the original cane.
STYLE.	The stem of the pistil that joins the stigma to the ovary.
SUCKERS.	Shoots or stems that arise from below the budhead, from the rootstock or from secondary crown on root surfaces below soil surface.
SUCKING INSECTS.	Types that feed by sucking the plant's juice or cell contents.
TINT.	The light tones of a hue.
TONE.	The lightness or darkness of a hue.
TRAILER.	A long-stemmed rose whose tendency is to grow over the ground, and which is therefore difficult to train upward against a support, as may be done with true climbers.
TRANSVERSE CUT.	A crosswise cut made horizontal to, or at right angles from, the direction of growth of a cut cane.
TREE ROSE.	A single stem topped with a crown of foliage or flowers. Same as a *standard rose*.
TWIG.	A smaller, usually many-jointed cane, growing laterally to the main canes of the rose bush's top.
UNION.	The point where the bud and rootstock are joined together.
VARIETY.	A rose within a species or type, but having some identifying characteristic of its own, perhaps color.
WEEPING STANDARDS.	Rambler roses budded on about 5-foot stems from which the top growth is trained to hang down or weep so that they would appear to be of a pendulous habit.
WHORLED.	Herein refers to the more or less circular pattern of buds at successive nodes on the rose cane. Same as *rosette of buds*.

INDEX